Excel
Basic Skills

Year 4
Ages 9–10

English

Get the Results You Want!

PASCAL PRESS

Tanya Dalgleish

Contents

Introduction

The aim of the ***Excel*** **Basic Skills English** series is to build on and reinforce students' basic skills in English. Each book in the series supports the requirements of Australian Curriculum English at each year level.

The ***Excel*** **Basic Skills English** series consists of seven books, one for each year level, from Kindergarten/Foundation to Year 6. The series is supported by other books in the ***Excel*** **Basic Skills** and **Advanced Skills** series.

Structure of the book

This book contains:

- thirty carefully graded, double-page units of teaching and learning activities
  - **Unit A** includes a sample informative, imaginative or persuasive text on subject matter relevant to a range of curriculum areas, and deals with **Reading and Comprehension skills**.
  - **Unit B** deals with the language conventions of **Spelling, Vocabulary, Grammar and Punctuation**.
- four double-page **revision units**.
- four double-page **NAPLAN-style Tests**.

How to use this book

- Students should complete one unit per week. A suggested plan would be to complete the Unit A page for the week on one day and the Unit B page on another day of the same week.
- At the end of a sequence of units students should undertake the applicable Revision units. If students find particular revision questions difficult they should revisit those areas in the previous sequence of units.
- After appropriate revision activities students should undertake the NAPLAN-style Test for those units. The revision work and testing should be completed on different days.

How to use this book with the *Excel* Basic Skills Mathematics series

For a complete **weekly English and Mathematics program** use this book in conjunction with the ***Excel*** *Basic Skills Mathematics Year 4* book. This way a student will have work set for four days a week—two days for English and two days for Mathematics.

How to assess students' progress

- Templates are included in each book of the series that outline the knowledge and skills targeted by the questions in that book. (Please see page 6.)
- The questions move through the subtopics of English in exactly the same order in each book but as there are more questions and more complex material included in later years of the Kindergarten/Foundation to Year 6 continuum, the question numbers vary across the books.
- The results of the work undertaken in each unit can be recorded on the marking grids. Please see the example on page 4. The marking grids on pages 6 and 7 are easy-to-use diagnostic tools that indicate where students' strengths and weaknesses lie in relation to specific areas of English. These results can be used to gather extra information about students' progress and their further revision needs.

The *Excel* Basic Skills and Advanced Skills series

If students are experiencing difficulty, require additional practice or need extension in any area of the course, further books are available to support them in the ***Excel*** **Basic Skills** and **Advanced Skills** series. (Please see the comprehensive list of ***Excel*** books on page 5.)

The *Excel* step-by-step improvement plan

Step 1

Read the introduction on page 3.

Step 2

Read this page, along with the marking grids and question templates on pages 6 and 7.

- **Question templates**
  These outline the knowledge and skills targeted by the questions in the book.
  Remember that the questions move through the subtopics of English in exactly the same order in each unit of the book.
- **Marking grids**
  The results of the work undertaken in each unit can be recorded on the marking grids.
  These are an easy-to-use diagnostic tool that indicate where each student's strengths and weaknesses are in relation to specific areas of English.
  These results can be used to gather extra information about each student's progress and their further revision needs. For example, see the sample marking grid in the right-hand column:
  - If a student is consistently getting more than one in five questions wrong in any topic, they need help in this area.
  - When marking answers on the grid, simply mark incorrect answers with 'X' in the appropriate box. This will result in a graphical representation of areas needing further work. An example for the first five units is shown above. If a question has several parts, it should be counted as wrong if one or more mistakes are made.
  - Remember that you can identify exactly what type of questions a student is having difficulty with in a topic. For example, in the grid above the student is having difficulty with Reading and Comprehension inferring questions.

	Literal	Literal	Inferring	Inferring	Evaluative	Evaluative
Question	**1**	**2**	**3**	**4**	**5**	**6**
Unit 1			X			
Unit 2				X		
Unit 3						
Unit 4				X		
Unit 5			X	X		
Unit 6						
Unit 7						
Unit 8						
Unit 9						
Unit 10						

This grid indicates that the student needs extra help and practice in inferring questions.

Step 3

Refer to page 5: ***Excel* books to help you *get the results you want*!**

- Under each topic there is a comprehensive list of books in our range to help students.
  For example, if a student wants help with Reading and Comprehension inferring questions or is ready to move on to more challenging work, the books shown at the top of the next page will help them.
  Each ***Excel*** book has a comprehensive contents page that will help you find the appropriate pages in the book to target the specific topic you want in each subject area.

Excel books to help you *get the results you want!*

Reading and Comprehension

Excel **Basic Skills**

9781741251661

9781864412796

Excel **Advanced Skills**

9781741254532

Excel **NAPLAN*-style Tests**

9781741254174

9781741253870

Spelling

Excel **Basic Skills**

9781864412826

Excel **Advanced Skills**

9781741252668

Excel **Handbooks and Guides**

9781864410617

Excel **NAPLAN*-style Tests**

9781741254174

9781741253870

Vocabulary

Excel **Basic Skills**

9781864412826

Excel **Basic Skills**

9781741251630

Excel **Advanced Skills**

9781864410600

Excel **NAPLAN*-style Tests**

9781741254174

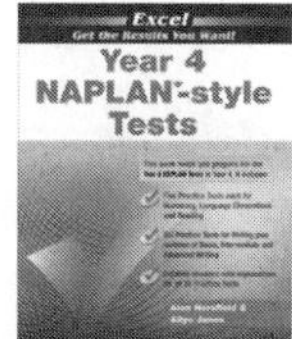

9781741253870

Grammar

Excel **Basic Skills**

9781864412840

Excel **Advanced Skills**

9781741254006

Excel **Handbooks and Guides**

9781864410600

Excel **NAPLAN*-style Tests**

9781741254174

9781741253870

Punctuation

Excel **Basic Skills**

9781864412840

Excel **Advanced Skills**

9781741254006

Excel **NAPLAN*-style Tests**

9781741254174

Excel **NAPLAN*-style Tests**

9781741253870

Writing

Excel **Basic Skills**

9781740200462

Excel **Advanced Skills**

9781741254044

General

Excel **Basic Skills Core**

9781864412758

Excel **Basic Skills**

9781741251579

Reading and Comprehension — QUESTION TEMPLATES

1–2 **Literal** Answers to these questions are found directly in the text.

3–4 **Inferring** Answers to these questions need to be worked out from clues in the text.

5–6 **Evaluative** Answers to these questions rely on making judgements about information in the text and beyond the text.

Spelling

1–4 **Proofreading**
In these questions, students use their understanding of spelling patterns and spelling rules to correct the spelling mistakes.

5 **Word families**
In this question, students use their understanding of base words, morphemes, prefixes, suffixes and etymology to create word families.

Vocabulary

6–9 **Synonyms, meaning in context, definitions**
Students need to comprehend the meaning of words in context to answer these vocabulary questions.

10–11 **Antonyms**
Students need to understand synonyms and antonyms to answer these vocabulary questions.

Grammar

12 **Nouns/Noun groups/Pronouns**
This question deals with aspects of a noun group, e.g. nouns, adjectives and articles.

13 **Verbs/Verb groups/Verb tense/Subject–verb agreement**
This question deals with different kinds of verbs: action (doing), thinking, saying, relating (being or having).

14 **Adverbials**
This question deals with adverbials, e.g. words and phrases that tell where, when and how.

15 **Cohesion**
This question deals with ways to link ideas across a text, e.g. conjunctions, connectives, pronouns.

Punctuation

16–18 **Proofreading**
These questions deal with aspects of punctuation for different kinds of sentences, including quoted (direct) and reported speech.

Reading and Comprehension — MARKING GRID

	Literal	Literal	Inferring	Inferring	Evaluative	Evaluative
Question	**1**	**2**	**3**	**4**	**5**	**6**
Unit 1						
Unit 2						
Unit 3						
Unit 4						
Unit 5						
Unit 6						
Unit 7						
Unit 8						
Unit 9						
Unit 10						
Unit 11						
Unit 12						
Unit 13						
Unit 14						
Unit 15						
Unit 16						
Unit 17						
Unit 18						
Unit 19						
Unit 20						
Unit 21						
Unit 22						
Unit 23						
Unit 24						
Unit 25						
Unit 26						
Unit 27						
Unit 28						
Unit 29						
Unit 30						
Question	**1**	**2**	**3**	**4**	**5**	**6**

Conventions of Language

MARKING GRID

	Spelling					Vocabulary						Grammar				Punctuation		
	Proofreading	Proofreading	Proofreading	Proofreading	Word families	Synonyms	Synonyms	Meaning in context	Definitions	Antonyms	Antonyms	Nouns/Noun groups/Pronouns	Verbs/Verb groups/ Verb tense/Subject-verb agreement	Adverbials	Cohesion	Proofreading	Proofreading	Proofreading
Question	**1**	**2**	**3**	**4**	**5**	**6**	**7**	**8**	**9**	**10**	**11**	**12**	**13**	**14**	**15**	**16**	**17**	**18**
Unit 1																		
Unit 2																		
Unit 3																		
Unit 4																		
Unit 5																		
Unit 6																		
Unit 7																		
Unit 8																		
Unit 9																		
Unit 10																		
Unit 11																		
Unit 12																		
Unit 13																		
Unit 14																		
Unit 15																		
Unit 16																		
Unit 17																		
Unit 18																		
Unit 19																		
Unit 20																		
Unit 21																		
Unit 22																		
Unit 23																		
Unit 24																		
Unit 25																		
Unit 26																		
Unit 27																		
Unit 28																		
Unit 29																		
Unit 30																		
Question	**1**	**2**	**3**	**4**	**5**	**6**	**7**	**8**	**9**	**10**	**11**	**12**	**13**	**14**	**15**	**16**	**17**	**18**

UNIT **1A**

Reading and Comprehension

Wear your helmet

'Daniella! Make sure you wear your helmet,' Mum yelled as Dani rushed out through the front door. She was on her way to the skate park to meet her friends.

'Yes, always,' she called back.

I know Daniella wears her helmet because I've seen her. But Mum has seen Dani's friends skateboarding without a helmet so Mum worries. Mum says some teenage boys and girls don't wear a helmet because it mucks up their hair. Mum also says that some teenagers like to think they are tough. They think that wearing a helmet makes them look weak. Dani's not like that. She always wears a helmet. She says, 'I need my brain so I need to protect it.'

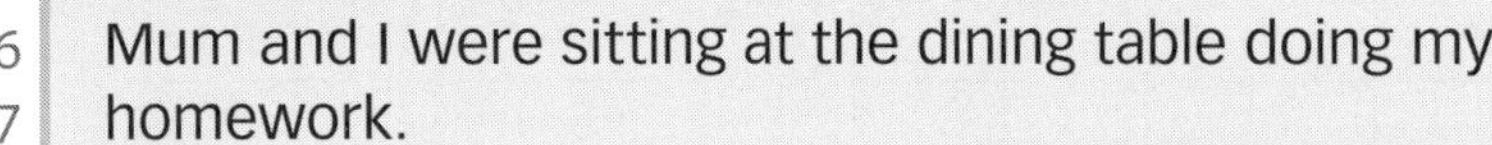

Mum and I were sitting at the dining table doing my homework.

I think it's stupid not to wear a helmet. I said, 'Don't worry, Mum. Dani's really sensible.'

'I know but I still worry.'

1 Why does Daniella wear a helmet?

- **A** to look cool
- **B** to protect her brain
- **C** to make Mum happy
- **D** to be sensible

2 Why was Dani rushing out?

- **A** to get out of doing homework
- **B** to get away from Mum
- **C** to meet her friends
- **D** to sneak out without a helmet

3 'I know but I still worry.' Who said this?

- **A** Dani
- **B** Daniella
- **C** the narrator
- **D** Mum

4 Which is true?

- **A** Dani and Mum argue about the helmet.
- **B** Dani's friends tell her to wear her helmet.
- **C** Dani cares more about her brain than her hair.
- **D** Dani worries about her hair.

5 The narrator thinks Dani is

- **A** sneaky.
- **B** a teenager.
- **C** stupid.
- **D** smart.

6 What does the narrator think about helmets?

....

....

Spelling

Rewrite the misspelt words.

1 Make sure you where your helmet.

....

2 Dani went to meet her frends.

....

3 Mum worries about safty.

....

4 Dani's really sensable.

....

5 Write new words using the correct suffix from the box.

s	es

helmet ....

worry ....

Vocabulary

Circle the word that has the nearest meaning to the underlined word.

6 Mum is worried about Dani's safety.

A nagging **B** concerned
C bothered **D** annoyed

7 Dani wears a helmet to protect her brain.

A shelter **B** hinder
C guard **D** neglect

8 Add a word from the text to the sentence.

Knee pads .... your knees.

9 Write a word from the text to match the meaning.

something that protects your head in an accident ....

Circle the word on each line that does **not** belong.

10 sensible clever smart stupid

11 safety danger hazard risk

Grammar

12 Complete the sentence with a common noun from the text.

A helmet protects your

....

13 Complete the sentence with an action (doing) verb from the text.

....

a helmet for protection in an accident.

14 Complete the sentence with an adverbial phrase from the text to tell **where**.

Mum was sitting

....

15 Use a connective from the box to complete the sentence correctly.

and	so	but	because	or

Wear a helmet ....

risk brain damage.

Punctuation

16 Circle the sentence that is punctuated correctly.

A 'yes, always,' she called back.
B 'Yes, always,' she called back.
C 'Yes, always' she called back.

Rewrite each sentence correctly.

17 dani needs her brain

....

....

18 I always wear a helmet said dani

....

....

Reading and Comprehension

Gorillas

Gorillas live in forests in Africa, in social groups called troops.

The adult male is called a silverback. He makes decisions and protects the troop.

Members of the troop help each other. They communicate through sounds, facial expression and body language. They bark if there's danger.

Young gorillas play rough games—practising to protect themselves.

When a gorilla dies the troop mourns.

GORILLAS
Endangered species

Gorillas sleep or rest during the day in nests made of foliage. Males nest on the ground and females on the ground or in trees; juveniles nest in trees and babies nest with their mums until they are about three.

Gorillas forage for food. They are herbivores and eat plants (mainly leaves and stems).

Some gorilla species eat a lot of fruit.

Leopards attack babies and youngsters.

Logging, civil war and mining destroys gorilla habitat.

Gorillas are killed for bushmeat or trade in gorilla parts.

1. A group of gorillas is a
   - A gang.
   - B group.
   - C troop.
   - D clan.

2. Where do gorillas sleep?
   - A in Africa
   - B in tunnels
   - C in the warm sun
   - D in nests

3. Choose all that apply. Gorillas are endangered because
   - A leopards kill them all.
   - B of habitat loss.
   - C people eat them.
   - D they fight each other.

4. What happens when a gorilla troop starts barking?
   - A They've seen a leopard.
   - B The gorillas hide in their nests.
   - C The silverback protects the troop.
   - D They forage for food.

5. Why does the silverback make decisions for the troop?
   - A He is the smartest gorilla.
   - B He can bark the loudest.
   - C He is a male.
   - D He is the boss.

6. Are gorillas sociable? Explain your answer.

....

....

....

Spelling

Rewrite the misspelt words.

1 Gorillas comunicate through sounds.

....

2 Gorillas are herbivors.

....

3 Some speecies eat a lot of fruit.

....

4 They are hunted for bushmeet.

....

5 Write new words using the correct suffix from the box.

s	es

gorilla ....

baby ....

Vocabulary

Circle the word that has the nearest meaning to the underlined word.

6 Gorillas forage for food.

- A hunt
- B scavenge
- C fight
- D dig

7 The silverback protects the troop.

- A grooms
- B disciplines
- C defends
- D approves

8 Add a word from the text to the sentence.

Young gorillas are sometimes .... by leopards.

9 Write a word from the text to match the meaning.

plant material ....

Circle the word on each line that does **not** belong.

10 protect attack defend shield

11 troop forest herd tribe

Grammar

12 Complete the sentence with a common noun from the text.

Young gorillas copy ....

13 Complete the sentence with an action (doing) verb from the text.

Gorillas .... leaves.

14 Complete the sentence with an adverbial phrase from the text to tell **where**.

Gorillas live ....

15 Use a connective from the box to complete the sentence correctly.

and	so	but	because	or

People kill gorillas for bushmeat

....

trade in gorilla parts.

Punctuation

16 Circle the sentence that is punctuated correctly.

- A Gorillas eat leaves, stems, shrubs, and vines.
- B Gorillas eat leaves stems shrubs and vines.
- C Gorillas eat leaves, stems, shrubs and vines.

Rewrite each sentence correctly.

17 gorillas bark if theres danger

....

....

18 a baby drinks its mothers milk

....

....

UNIT 3A

Reading and Comprehension

How the lizard got its spikes

One day a slinky-skinned lizard decided to practise throwing his boomerang. The boomerang came back to him each time he threw it. Lizard saw that a galah was watching him from a nearby tree. He felt very proud of himself.

Lizard started to show off for the galah, throwing the boomerang harder and harder. Then he threw the boomerang extra hard and gave it a twist. The boomerang whizzed through the air and curved back and scalped the galah on top of her head. The galah shrieked in agony. The boomerang had sliced off skin and feathers. She was bleeding badly. She shrieked and screamed and cawed and hopped around, knocking her head on the ground in her pain.

The frightened lizard hid behind a bindeah bush to watch but Galah spotted the lizard and grabbed him in her beak. She was stronger and so rolled him around in the bindeah bush until he was stuck all over in prickles. Then she rubbed her blood over him saying, 'You shall be covered in spikes and stained with my blood forever.'

And from that day forward the galah has had a bald spot under its crest and the lizard has been spiky and red.

Adapted from an Aboriginal folktale

1 What did the boomerang do to the galah?

- **A** It stuck in her head.
- **B** It knocked her out of the tree.
- **C** It scalped her.
- **D** It sliced her head off.

2 Which animal is stronger?

- **A** a bindeah
- **B** the galah
- **C** the lizard
- **D** a bird

3 Why was Lizard frightened?

- **A** Galahs hate lizards.
- **B** He knew Galah would be angry with him.
- **C** Galah was bleeding badly.
- **D** Galah was knocking her head on the ground.

4 Where did the lizard's spikes come from?

- **A** Bindeah bushes have thorns.
- **B** They grew on Lizard.
- **C** Lizard was covered with spikes.
- **D** Galah glued spikes onto Lizard.

5 Why did the accident happen?

- **A** Lizard was showing off.
- **B** Galah was in the way.
- **C** The boomerang didn't work properly.
- **D** Lizard wanted to hurt Galah.

6 Was Lizard's punishment fair? Explain.

Spelling

Rewrite the misspelt words.

1 Galah <u>wotched</u> from a tree.

....

2 Lizard felt <u>prowed</u> of himself.

....

3 Galah was <u>bleading</u>.

....

4 Galah has a <u>balled</u> spot.

....

5 Write new words using the correct suffix from the box.

ed	ing

throw ....

shriek ....

Vocabulary

Circle the word that has the nearest meaning to the underlined word.

6 You shall be <u>stained</u> with my blood.

A rolled **B** marked
C covered **D** stuck

7 Skin and feathers were <u>sliced</u> off.

A shared **B** pulled
C rubbed **D** scalped

8 Add a word from the text to the sentence.

Galah .... him in her beak.

9 Write a word from the text to match the meaning.

a curved flat piece of wood used for hunting ....

Circle the word on each line that does **not** belong.

10 agony pain happiness suffering

11 whispered shrieked screamed cawed

Grammar

12 Complete the sentence with a common noun from the text.

The galah grabbed the .... in her beak.

13 Complete the sentence with an action (doing) verb from the text.

He .... the boomerang extra hard.

14 Complete the sentence with an adverbial phrase from the text to tell **where**.

The boomerang whizzed ....

15 Use a connective from the box to complete the sentence correctly.

and	so	but	because	or

Galah has a bald spot

....

Lizard is spiky and red.

Punctuation

16 Circle the sentence that is punctuated correctly.

A he felt very proud of himself.
B He felt very proud of himself.
C ‘He’ felt very proud of himself.

Rewrite each sentence correctly.

17 galah shrieked and screamed

....

....

18 galah said you shall be covered in spikes

....

....

UNIT 4A

Reading and Comprehension

The Easter bilby

Bunnies have been associated with Easter eggs for hundreds of years. The idea of an Easter bunny delivering eggs comes from German folklore, which tells of a hare that judges whether or not children have been well-behaved.

Australia should use Easter bilbies instead of Easter bunnies. Bunnies (rabbits and hares) are not native to Australia. European rabbits arrived in Australia on the First Fleet. They are feral pests. They breed too easily and eat food that native animals need to survive. They are partly to blame for the extinction of several small Australian native mammals and are one reason why Australian animals such as the bilby are now endangered.

Some chocolate companies that sell Easter bilbies donate some of the purchase money towards projects to save the bilby. This is good. Be careful though to buy the right chocolate bilbies. Not all chocolate bilbies are made by companies that donate money to help bilby conservation.

Easter bilbies are better than Easter bunnies. Bilbies are Australian native animals.

By Jade, age 10

1. Why are rabbits bad for Australian native animals?
   - **A** They are feral pests.
   - **B** They eat all the native animals' food.
   - **C** They make cute chocolates.
   - **D** Children love them.

2. The writer says that bunnies are
   - **A** cute.
   - **B** pests.
   - **C** good at Easter time.
   - **D** good chocolates.

3. How did rabbits come to Australia?
   - **A** by plane
   - **B** as pets
   - **C** as pests
   - **D** by ship

4. In German folklore who decided if children had been well-behaved?
   - **A** their parents
   - **B** a judge
   - **C** a hare
   - **D** a bilby

5. Choose all that apply. Why is an Easter bunny a bad idea for Australia?
   - **A** Feral rabbits are a big problem in Australia.
   - **B** It's not good to promote rabbits as wonderful.
   - **C** Chocolate is unhealthy.
   - **D** People eat too much chocolate.

6. How can chocolate help bilbies?

   ....

   ....

Spelling

Rewrite the misspelt words.

1 A hare judges wether children have been good.

2 We shood have Easter bilbies.

3 Rabbits breed too easuly.

4 Be cairfull to buy the right bilby.

5 Write new words using the correct suffix from the box.

es	ing

bilby

donate

Vocabulary

Circle the word that has the nearest meaning to the underlined word.

6 We shouldn't promote feral animals.
A endorse B help
C reject D approve

7 Bilbies are Australian native animals.
A mammals B feral
C indigenous D wild

8 Add a word from the text to the sentence.
At Easter, eggs are made of ______.

9 Write a word from the text to match the meaning.
a person, animal or thing that causes a problem ______

Circle the word on each line that does **not** belong.

10 extinction death survival elimination

11 severe minor grave serious

Grammar

12 Complete the sentence with a common noun from the text.
There are ______ to save the bilby.

13 Complete the sentence with an action (doing) verb from the text.
Rabbits ______ too easily.

14 Complete the sentence with an adverbial phrase from the text to tell **where**.
Rabbits arrived ______ on the First Fleet.

15 Use a pronoun from the box to complete the sentence correctly.

he	she	it	you	they	I	we

Bilbies are better than bunnies because ______ are native animals.

Punctuation

16 Circle the sentence that is punctuated correctly.
A We shouldnt support Easter bunnies.
B we shouldn't support Easter bunnies.
C We shouldn't support Easter bunnies.

Rewrite each sentence correctly.

17 the easter bunny idea comes from german folklore

18 european rabbits came to australia on the first fleet.

Reading and Comprehension

Energy balls

An easy-to-make, tasty, sweet treat.
No cooking required.
Good for people with allergies. Free of gluten, dairy, egg and nuts.
Add to school lunches as a healthy snack.

INGREDIENTS

1 cup dates (pits removed)
$\frac{1}{2}$ cup shredded coconut
$\frac{1}{2}$ cup cocoa powder
juice and zest of half an orange
$\frac{1}{2}$ cup extra shredded coconut to coat the balls

METHOD

Add all ingredients to a food processor.
Process on high until combined. (Add a small amount of water if mixture is too thick to combine.)
Shape mixture into small balls.
Roll each ball in extra coconut to coat it.

1. Which ingredient has pits?
   - **A** coconut
   - **B** dates
   - **C** cocoa
   - **D** orange juice

2. What shape are the balls?
   - **A** square
   - **B** round
   - **C** logs
   - **D** blocks

3. Choose all that apply. Why are they easy to make?
   - **A** They don't need cooking.
   - **B** There are only four steps.
   - **C** There are only four ingredients.
   - **D** They are quick to make.

4. How do you know if the mixture is too thick?
   - **A** It needs water.
   - **B** It won't combine.
   - **C** You have to process the mix on high.
   - **D** It's lumpy.

5. Is it a child-friendly recipe?
   - **A** Yes. No cooking is required.
   - **B** No. You need to use a food processor.
   - **C** Yes. You don't need a sharp knife.
   - **D** No. Children won't like them.

6. Why is it described as a sweet treat?

Spelling

Rewrite the misspelt words.

1 Add a small ammount of water.

....

2 Energy balls are a helthy snack.

....

3 They are diary free.

....

4 Add orange joose.

....

5 Write new words using the correct suffix from the box.

es	ing

allergy ....

process ....

Vocabulary

Circle the word that has the nearest meaning to the underlined word.

6 Good for allergy sufferers.

A healthy **B** sweet
C tasty **D** suitable

7 Use extra shredded coconut to coat the balls.

A warm **B** wrap
C cover **D** conceal

8 Add a word from the text to the sentence.

We give the dog a .... when it obeys a command.

9 Write a word from the text to match the meaning.

the outer coloured part of an orange or lemon ....

Circle the word on each line that does **not** belong.

10 remove add delete eliminate

11 tasty delicious bitter flavoursome

Grammar

12 Complete the sentence with a common noun from the text.

Energy balls are a tasty

....

13 Complete the sentence with an action (doing) verb from the text.

....

to school lunch boxes.

14 Complete the sentence with an adverbial phrase from the text to tell **where**.

Roll each ball ....

15 Use a pronoun from the box to complete the sentence correctly.

he	she	it	you	they	I	we

Energy balls are my favourite treat.

....

love to snack on them.

Punctuation

16 Circle the sentence that is punctuated correctly.

A the recipe is for a tasty snack
B The recipe is for a tasty snack.
C the recipe is for a tasty snack.

Rewrite each sentence correctly.

17 linda said I like coconut

....

....

....

18 paul made a tasty snack

....

....

....

My weekend

Every Sunday my family and lots of our friends all drive down to the coast. It takes over an hour but we leave home really early and we don't come home until dark. On long weekends we stay until really late and buy fish and chips for dinner. Sometimes we don't get home until after 10 pm. Mum says that doesn't matter because there's no school the next day.

The park where we go is at a beach that has a safe area for swimming. There's also lots of playground equipment such as a slippery dip, swings, a rope climb and a flying fox. There're big trees for shade and we can cook our lunch on the council barbecue. We go swimming and play games. We take a rugby ball and play touch footy. There's also a sandpit with a volleyball net so we play volleyball too. That's my favourite. It's a lot of fun.

We always take our rubbish home with us. Mum keeps reminding us, 'We come here every Sunday because it's beautiful. We need to make sure it's still beautiful when we leave, and not trashed.' We all agree with that.

1. How long does it take to drive to the beach?
   - **A** an hour
   - **B** under an hour
   - **C** until dark
   - **D** over an hour

2. Which activity does the writer prefer?
   - **A** using the playground equipment
   - **B** touch football
   - **C** volleyball
   - **D** swimming

3. Mum
   - **A** is entertaining and funny.
   - **B** cares for the environment and likes to have fun.
   - **C** is a responsible citizen and strict about school.
   - **D** is good at volleyball and picking up trash.

4. Choose all that apply. The swimming area is safe from
   - **A** wild surf and sharks.
   - **B** boats.
   - **C** surf craft.
   - **D** lifesavers.

5. Rate the importance of the outing to the family from 1 to 4. 1 is for **not that important** and 4 is for **extremely important**.
   - **A** 1
   - **B** 2
   - **C** 3
   - **D** 4

6. How would you describe the family?

   ....

   ....

Spelling

Rewrite the misspelt words.

1 I have fun with my famly and friends.

....

2 Somtimes we go home after dark.

....

3 We swim at the beech.

....

4 Mum's favrit game is netball.

....

5 Write new words using the correct suffix from the box.

es	ing

remind ....

family ....

Vocabulary

Circle the word that has the nearest meaning to the underlined word.

6 The beach has a safe area for swimming.

A pool **B** patrolled
C open **D** protected

7 We always take our rubbish home with us.

A equipment **B** garbage
C litter **D** food

8 Add a word from the text to the sentence.
We enjoy Sundays with our family and

....

9 Write a word from the text to match the meaning.

an area of shelter from the sun

....

Circle the word on each line that does **not** belong.

10 trashed protected ruined wrecked

11 beautiful spoilt natural lovely

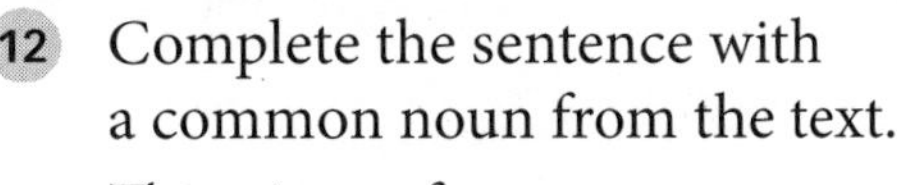

Grammar

12 Complete the sentence with a common noun from the text.

There is a safe ....
for swimming.

13 Complete the sentence with an action (doing) verb from the text.

We like to ....
games.

14 Complete the sentence with an adverbial phrase from the text to tell **where**.

We cook lunch ....

15 Use a pronoun from the box to complete the sentence correctly.

he	she	it	you	they	I	we

We love the beach because

....

is beautiful.

Punctuation

16 Circle the sentence that is punctuated correctly.

A Therere big trees for shade.
B Therere big trees for shade
C There're big trees for shade.

Rewrite each sentence correctly.

17 mum said pick up the rubbish

....

....

....

18 theres no surf so its very safe

....

....

....

Reading and Comprehension

Be considerate

Dad says,
'Cycling on the road
can be dangerous.
Drivers sometimes drive
in the bicycle lane.
They don't know the rules
for sharing the road
with bicycles.'

Uncle says,
'Sharing a footpath
with a dog
can be dangerous.
Some dogs run across
in front of you.
Some dog owners don't have
any sense.'

I say,
'Sometimes cycling
on the footpath
is dangerous.
People
block the path.
They don't know the rules
for sharing with bicycles.'

Grandma says,
'Walking on a shared path
can be dangerous.'
Grandma tells us,
'I stick to the left.
I give way.
I share the footpath
with everyone.'

1. How many people give opinions in the poem?
   - **A** one
   - **B** two
   - **C** three
   - **D** four

2. What does Uncle worry about?
   - **A** people
   - **B** dogs
   - **C** bicycles
   - **D** cars

3. Who cycles in the poem?
   - **A** the poet and Dad
   - **B** Uncle, Dad and the poet
   - **C** Uncle and Dad
   - **D** all of the people

4. What can be dangerous about a footpath?
   - **A** bikes
   - **B** dogs
   - **C** bikes and dogs
   - **D** bikes, dogs, people

5. Who is the most considerate person?
   - **A** Dad
   - **B** Uncle
   - **C** the poet
   - **D** Grandma

6. Write a fifth stanza for the poem. Give your opinion about cycling or sharing the footpath.

   ....

   ....

   ....

Spelling

Rewrite the misspelt words.

1 Follow the rools.

2 Dad rides a bycicle.

3 Cycling can be dangerus.

4 Some peeple block the path.

5 Write new words using the correct suffix from the box.

ed	ing

say

cycle

Vocabulary

Circle the word that has the nearest meaning to the underlined word.

6 Cycling can be dangerous.
A tricky
B difficult
C scary
D deadly

7 There are rules for footpath use.
A problems
B guidelines
C decisions
D arguments

8 Add a word from the text to the sentence.
Sometimes ______ on the footpath is dangerous.

9 Write a word from the text to match the meaning.
to be thoughtful of others ______

Circle the word on each line that does **not** belong.

10 intelligence humour sense judgement

11 block assist obstruct hinder

Grammar

12 Complete the sentence with a common noun from the text.
______ sometimes drive in the cycle lane.

13 Complete the sentence with an action (doing) verb from the text.
______ the footpath with everyone.

14 Complete the sentence with an adverbial phrase from the text to tell **where**.
Cycling ______ can be dangerous.

15 Use a pronoun from the box to complete the sentence correctly.

he	she	it	you	they	I	we

Grandma sticks to the left because ______ knows the rules.

Punctuation

16 Circle the sentence that is punctuated correctly.
A Uncle says, 'Some dog owners have no sense.'
B Uncle says 'Some dog owners have no sense.'
C Uncle says, Some dog owners have no sense.

Rewrite each sentence correctly.

17 I love cycling said dad

18 grandma says stick to the left

Reading and Comprehension

Write a common noun from the box in each space.

troop	bicycle	gorilla	brain	leopard
silverback	bilbies	skateboard	bunnies	important

1 Wearing a helmet protects your ____________________ in an accident. It's ____________________ to wear a helmet when you ride a ____________________ or a ____________________.

2 A ____________________ will bark if a ____________________ is near. The ____________________ protects the ____________________.

3 In Australia we should have Easter ____________________ instead of Easter ____________________.

Write a common noun from the box in each space.

rubbish	nuts	zest	eggs	shade	rules	safety	dairy	orange	equipment

4 The juice and ____________________ of an ____________________ adds flavour to sweet treats.

5 Some people are allergic to ____________________, ____________________ or ____________________.

6 Some parks have lots of fun playground ____________________. Trees provide ____________________ in parks. It's important not to leave ____________________ behind in parks.

7 When using a shared footpath, there are ____________________ for people's ____________________.

Spelling

The spelling mistakes in these sentences have been circled. Write the correct spelling on the lines.

8 It's fun to play with (freinds). ____________________

9 Mum and Dad worry about bike (safty). ____________________

10 Gorillas (comunicate) with each other. ____________________

11 Gorillas are (herbavors). ____________________

12 Lizard felt (prowd) of himself. ____________________

13 Be (cairfull) when cycling. ____________________

14 Eat (helthy) snacks. ____________________

15 My (favrit) game is volleyball. ____________________

Vocabulary

16 Circle the correct word in the brackets.

The (whether / weather) was fine last Sunday.

17 Circle the word that means the opposite of **danger**.

safety   deadly   protect

Grammar

18 Add a common noun to the sentence.

Gorillas sleep in ______________________________.

19 Add a verb to the sentence.

Gorillas ______________________________ plants.

20 Add an adverbial phrase to tell **where**.

Rabbits arrived ______________________________ on the First Fleet.

21 Add a pronoun to the sentence.

Roll each ball in extra coconut to coat ______________________________.

22 Add a connective to the sentence.

Take your rubbish home ______________________________ the beach stays beautiful.

Punctuation

Rewrite each sentence correctly.

23 david said I love the beach

____

____

24 the easter bunny idea comes from german folklore

____

____

25 grandma said share the footpath

____

____

Reading

Why cats kill rats

A long time ago there was a very wealthy king. The king employed a cat to manage his warehouse. The king employed a rat to assist the cat.

The rat loved a girl who worked in the king's kitchen. The rat was too poor to buy her gifts so he decided to sneak into the king's warehouse and steal something to give her. He stole corn and native pears. He gave them to his sweetheart.

At the end of the month when the cat checked supplies in the warehouse she noticed that some corn and native pears were missing. She asked the kitchen staff if they knew anything. She was told that the rat was the thief.

The cat reported the theft to the king. The king was angry about being betrayed. As punishment he dismissed the kitchen girl and the cat and he told the cat to deal with the rat. The cat was so angry with the rat that she killed it and ate it.

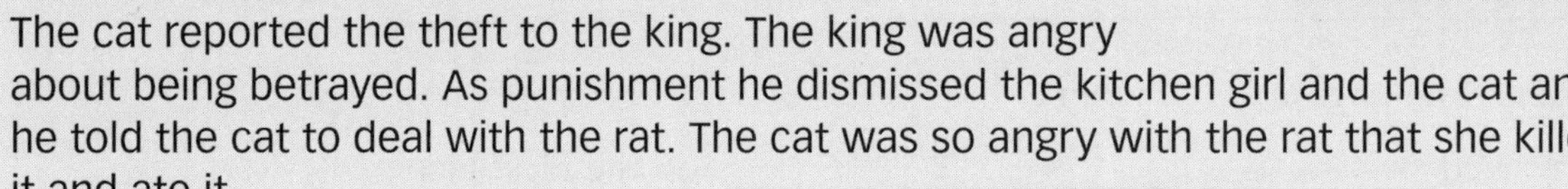

And, from that day forward, cats have always killed rats.

Adapted from a Nigerian folktale

1. How did the cat find the thief?
   - **A** The king told the cat.
   - **B** She asked the kitchen staff.
   - **C** She caught the thief in the warehouse.
   - **D** The girl told on the rat.

2. What did the rat steal?
   - **A** lots of things to eat
   - **B** any kind of gifts
   - **C** corn and native pears
   - **D** his sweetheart's love

3. How often did the cat check the warehouse?
   - **A** not very often
   - **B** once a month
   - **C** every day
   - **D** once in a while

4. Choose all that apply. Who betrayed whom?
   - **A** The king betrayed the cat.
   - **B** The rat betrayed the cat.
   - **C** The rat betrayed the king.
   - **D** The girl betrayed the rat.

5. Choose all that apply. The cat killed the rat
   - **A** because that's what cats do.
   - **B** to punish it.
   - **C** because she was so angry.
   - **D** because the king had said to.

6. Choose all that apply. The girl lost her job because the king thought
   - **A** the kitchen staff did not like her.
   - **B** she had accepted stolen goods.
   - **C** she loved the rat.
   - **D** she should have reported the rat.

7. Which statement or statements do you agree with?
   - **A** The king was mean.
   - **B** The cat should not have been punished.
   - **C** The cat deserved to be punished.
   - **D** The rat was a fool.

NAPLAN-STYLE

1

CONVENTIONS OF LANGUAGE TEST

Spelling

The spelling mistakes in these sentences have been underlined.
Write the correct spelling on the lines.

1 The rat decided to <u>steel</u> things. ______________________

2 The king <u>punisht</u> everyone. ______________________

3 The rat was a <u>theef</u>. ______________________

4 The girl <u>werked</u> in the kitchen. ______________________

Vocabulary

5 Which word means **goods stored in a warehouse**?

A food B supplies C packages D deliveries

6 Which word does **not** belong?

A employees B staff C king D workers

7 Which word does **not** belong?

A sacked B dismissed C employed D unemployed

Grammar

8 Which adjective describes how the cat felt at the end?

A sad B sorry C angry D proud

9 Which verb tells what the cat did to the rat?

A employed B dismissed C loved D killed

10 Which adverbial phrase tells **where** the supplies were kept?

A in the king's kitchen B in the warehouse C through the roof D at the end

Punctuation

11 Which sentence is punctuated correctly?

A The rat assisted, the cat.
B The rat stole from the king's warehouse.
C The rat stole the kings pears.
D The rat was in love

12 Which sentence is punctuated correctly?

A The king doe'snt care about the cat.
B The king, cares about his pears.
C The king doesn't care about the cat.
D The kings staff must be loyal.

Reading and Comprehension

Blog

What will you be doing next Earth Day, 22 April?

▾ **Posted** on 17 January **1079 comments**

The first Earth Day was in 1970. Twenty million people took part. Now more than one billion people participate in Earth Day activities around the globe every year. Earth Day is a special day. It focuses our attention on caring for the earth.

Next Earth Day join the fight against climate change. Great Earth Day activities include planting trees, promoting recycling, volunteering locally for green projects and cutting down on the amount of energy you use. You can walk or cycle instead of taking the car, pick up litter when you see it, use a refillable water bottle made of stainless steel instead of a single-use plastic bottle. You can refuse to buy plastic and bring your own bags to the grocery store. You can eat less meat to help reduce greenhouse gas emissions.

Earth Day is supported by a number of celebrities, including Leonardo DiCaprio, Emma Watson, Miley Cyrus and Matt Damon.

1 When was the first Earth Day?

- **A** 22 April
- **B** 1970
- **C** next Earth Day
- **D** every year

2 How many people participate in Earth Day?

- **A** more than a billion
- **B** one billion
- **C** millions
- **D** one million

3 How does walking or cycling help the earth?

- **A** It is good exercise.
- **B** It is healthier for you.
- **C** It reduces traffic congestion.
- **D** It saves energy.

4 Why should you use a refillable stainless steel water bottle?

- **A** It's useful for when you are thirsty.
- **B** It reduces plastic pollution.
- **C** It keeps water colder.
- **D** It's lighter to carry.

5 Why is it good to have celebrities involved? Choose all that apply.

- **A** They bring star power.
- **B** They draw media attention.
- **C** If you like the celebrity you are more likely to support the cause.
- **D** People tend to copy what their favourite celebrities do.

6 Why is there need of an Earth Day?

....

....

Spelling

Rewrite the misspelt words.

1 Twentee million people took part.

2 It's important to recycal.

3 Yoose refillable water bottles.

4 Earth Day is a spechal day.

5 Write new words using the correct prefix from the box.

un	re	mis	im

fillable ______

caring ______

Vocabulary

Circle the word that has the nearest meaning to the underlined word.

6 Activities include promoting recycling.

A supporting B using
C doing D opposing

7 Fight against climate change.

A join B argue
C battle D work

8 Add a word from the text to the sentence.

Eat less meat to ______ greenhouse gases.

9 Write a word from the text to match the meaning.

giving your time for free ______

Circle the word on each line that does **not** belong.

10 participate observe engage contribute

11 neglect attention thoughtfulness consideration

Grammar

12 Complete the sentence with an adjective (describing word) from the text.

Earth Day is a ______ day.

13 Complete the sentence with a thinking verb from the text.

Earth Day ______ attention on the Earth.

14 Complete the sentence with an adverbial phrase from the text to tell **when**.

The first Earth Day was ______.

15 Use a connective from the box to complete the sentence correctly.

When	Then	While	Next	Eventually

______ Earth Day we will plant trees with Landcare.

Punctuation

16 Circle the sentence that is punctuated correctly.

A Emma Watson supports Earth Day.
B Emma watson supports earth day.
C Emma Watson supports Earth day.

Rewrite each sentence correctly.

17 lots of celebrities support earth day

18 earth day and anzac day are both special

Reading and Comprehension

What's in an ad?

Name: *Ivy*

I noticed an advertisement for *breakfast cereal.*

This advertisement caught my attention because *firstly, it had good music, and then I saw that the family was eating breakfast and they looked extremely happy. After breakfast the children went to play with their friends. The children in the ad were all healthy-looking and happy. They were laughing, smiling, playing and having fun.*

This ad was aimed at *children.*

The message in the ad was that *happy smiling families eat this cereal for breakfast and when you eat it you will be healthy, have lots of energy and you will be popular.*

The ad was misleading because *breakfast cereal cannot make you or your family happy or help you make friends.*

Conclusion: *The advertisement made me want to buy the product because it showed children having fun. This ad is misleading for two reasons. Firstly, I know that in real life breakfast cereal doesn't make people have more fun. Secondly, when I read the cereal box at the supermarket, the cereal was 28% sugar so I know it is not healthy.*

1 What was the advertisement for?
- A a happy family
- B breakfast cereal
- C exercise
- D having fun

2 Choose all that apply. The ad tells viewers that the cereal will make them
- A healthy.
- B popular.
- C have fun.
- D happy.

3 The advertisement was
- A on the radio.
- B on television.
- C in the newspaper.
- D on the side of a bus.

4 What did the writer like most about the ad?
- A the happy family
- B the breakfast cereal
- C the music
- D the children playing

5 How truthful did the writer think the ad was?
- A not very
- B fairly truthful
- C totally truthful
- D totally untruthful

6 Who might buy the product advertised?

Spelling

Rewrite the misspelt words.

1 The ad had good musik.

2 The family was eating brekfast.

3 The children were larfing.

4 This ad is misleading for two reasins.

5 Write new words using the correct prefix from the box.

un	re	mis	im

healthy

leading

Vocabulary

Circle the word that has the nearest meaning to the underlined word.

6 Most children want to be popular.
A well-liked **B** friendly
C happy **D** playful

7 In real life cereal doesn't give people better lives.
A fantasy **B** television
C fictional **D** true

8 Add a word from the text to the sentence.
Cereal is sold in a .

9 Write a word from the text to match the meaning.
grains such as wheat, corn or rice, used for food

Circle the word on each line that does **not** belong.

10 misleading honest deceptive dishonest

11 happy depressed laughing playful

Grammar

12 Complete the sentence with an adjective from the text.
This advertisement is
for two reasons.

13 Complete the sentence with a thinking verb from the text.
I sugar is not healthy.

14 Complete the sentence with an adverbial phrase from the text to tell **when**.
the children went to play outdoors.

15 Use a connective from the box to complete the sentence correctly.

when	then	while	next	eventually

I heard good music and

I saw the family was eating breakfast.

Punctuation

16 Circle the sentence that is punctuated correctly.
A This advertising isnt truthful.
B This advertising isn't truthful
C This advertising isn't truthful.

Rewrite each sentence correctly.

17 breakfast cereal doesnt make people happy

18 the children were laughing smiling and playing

What am I?

What am I?
I have
feathered wings to fly
but I will never
soar
through the sky.
I have eyes
to see the trees
but I will never
rest
in their branches.
I have a heart
that wants a mate
but I will never
make a nest
or be a pair.

All I have is time,
extending
behind
and
stretching
in front.
But will I
have time
to be me
and do the things
I was born to do?
I am a bird
looking out
through bars.
I wish
…

1. Where is the bird?
   - **A** in a tree
   - **B** in a nest
   - **C** in a zoo
   - **D** in a cage

2. Where will the bird never rest?
   - **A** in the sky
   - **B** in a nest
   - **C** in a tree
   - **D** in a cage

3. Why will the bird never be a pair?
   - **A** It lives alone.
   - **B** It's searching for a mate.
   - **C** Its mate is dead.
   - **D** There's no time.

4. What was the bird born to do?
   - **A** fly through the sky
   - **B** fly, see the trees, be a pair
   - **C** fly, nest in a tree, find a mate
   - **D** soar, be a pair

5. How does the bird feel? Choose all that apply.
   - **A** sad
   - **B** frightened
   - **C** bored
   - **D** lonely

6. Does the bird wish for something impossible?

Spelling

Rewrite the misspelt words.

1 Caged birds can't soar threw the sky.

2 The bird has a hart that wants a mate.

3 Time is streching out in front of the bird.

4 A set of two things is a pear.

5 Write new words using the correct prefix from the box.

un	re	mis	im

do

possible

Vocabulary

Circle the word that has the nearest meaning to the underlined word.

6 I will never soar through the sky.
A drift B climb
C fly D float

7 I have a heart that wants a mate.
A mother B child
C companion D father

8 Add a word from the text to the sentence.
A cage has .

9 Write a word from the text to match the meaning.
These support birds and aircraft in flight.

Circle the word on each line that does **not** belong.

10 feathered scaly furry beak

11 nest baby burrow den

Grammar

12 Complete the sentence with an adjective from the text.
The bird has wings to fly.

13 Complete the sentence with a thinking verb from the text.
I I could fly.

14 Complete the sentence with an adverbial phrase to tell **where**.
The bird looks out .

15 Use a connective from the box to complete the sentence correctly.

when	then	while	next	eventually

The bird will never fly through the sky

it lives in a cage.

Punctuation

16 Circle the sentence that is punctuated correctly.
A The bird can't have a mate.
B The bird cant have a mate.
C The bird cant have a mate

Rewrite each sentence correctly.

17 what am I asked the bird

18 the bird couldnt fly

Reading and Comprehension

Timeline
About
Notes
Photos
More

Lost and found pets

Like Message

Helpful tips to find your loved ones.

Pet service—Community organisation

Search for posts on this page

FOUND wandering alone on Palm Avenue, Friday—hungry, very friendly, no collar ... *See more*

MISSING DOG—Doug messaged for the owner. Hi, I'm just at Rainbow Beach and a lady has lost her dachshund! It wriggled off its leash and ran to the beach! Its name is Chorizo. If anyone sees it, please contact us. The owner is very distraught.

I've got the dachshund. Meet me at ... *See more*

WHITE PERSIAN CAT—spotted on Whitby Street, Trentwood. My dog woke me at around 1:30 am. I think he was barking at a cat that had been hanging around our backyard. Sorry, I couldn't catch the cat.

MISSING—female tabby—Southport. Loopy Lou was chased by nasty dog at Mabel Crescent, Labrador, on Wednesday afternoon and I haven't seen her since. Missing her very much ... *See more*

MISSING—Blue budgie lost in Sorrento. Flew towards the racecourse. If sighted contact Amy ... *See more*

1 Who lost a blue budgie?
- A Chorizo
- B Doug
- C Amy
- D Mabel

2 Loopy Lou is a
- A dog owner.
- B tabby cat.
- C blue budgie.
- D white Persian.

3 What is the purpose of the website?
- A to find lost people
- B to help pets find owners
- C to report missing and found pets
- D to advertise pets

4 What is a community organisation?
- A an organisation run by the government
- B an internet organisation
- C a community shop
- D a group that helps members of a community

5 How does Doug feel about Chorizo?
- A caring
- B sad
- C distraught
- D frantic

6 Would this website be useful? Explain.

....

....

....

....

Spelling

Rewrite the misspelt words.

1 The dog was hungrey.

2 The dog wriggeld off its leash.

3 Loopy Lou went missing on Wensday.

4 Loopy Lou was chast by a dog.

5 Write three words from the word family that includes **wander**.

Vocabulary

Circle the word that has the nearest meaning to the underlined word.

6 Chorizo's owner is distraught.
A distant B puzzled
C distressed D calm

7 The dog was very friendly.
A aggressive B sociable
C quiet D standoffish

8 Add a word from the text to the sentence.
When you help someone you provide ____________.

9 Write a word from the text to match the meaning.
a rope or strap used to walk a dog or other animal ____________

Circle the word on each line that does **not** belong.

10 search hunt seek hide

11 treasured loved despised valued

Grammar

12 Complete the sentence with an adjective from the text.
Loopy Loo was chased by a ____________ dog.

13 Complete the sentence with a thinking verb from the text.
I ____________ my dog was barking at a cat.

14 Complete the sentence with an adverbial phrase from the text to tell **when**.
My dog woke me ____________.

15 Use a connective from the box to complete the sentence correctly.

When	Then	While	Next	Eventually

Everyone searched.

____

Loopy Lou returned home on her own.

Punctuation

16 Circle the sentence that is punctuated correctly.
A Its name is Chorizo?
B It's name is chorizo.
C Its name is Chorizo.

Rewrite each sentence correctly.

17 Im at rainbow beach

18 amy lost her budgie in sorrento

Reading and Comprehension

Wild animals are not pets

The slow loris is a nocturnal rainforest mammal. It sleeps in the trees all day and is active at night. It is small and cute. It can use both hands to eat while hanging upside down from a branch.

The slow loris makes a toxin in a gland on its arm. When it licks the gland, saliva activates the toxin. It licks its fur during grooming and covers itself with the toxin to deter predators. The slow loris will bite if it's frightened. Bites are toxic because of the toxin in the saliva.

In markets in Asia people can buy a slow loris for a pet. These animals have been stolen from the forest. Their teeth are pulled out so they can't bite anyone. It is very painful for lorises to have their teeth pulled out. Many bleed to death or die from infection afterwards. Many also die as pets because they are not fed their proper forest foods.

Slow lorises belong in the wild. I believe it is very cruel to keep them as pets. People should not buy any wild animal for a pet. If no-one bought them, then poachers would not steal them from the wild. By Molly, age nine

1. Where are slow lorises from?
   - **A** Asia
   - **B** Australia
   - **C** cages
   - **D** trees

2. When do slow lorises like to be active?
   - **A** any time
   - **B** in the day
   - **C** in the night
   - **D** when it's light

3. Molly wrote the text to tell people
   - **A** what slow lorises look like.
   - **B** about pets.
   - **C** not to buy wild animals as pets.
   - **D** how slow lorises live.

4. What is a 'poacher' in the text?
   - **A** someone who keeps a loris as a pet
   - **B** a farmer
   - **C** someone who steals animals from the wild
   - **D** a pet seller

5. How does Molly feel about slow lorises as pets?
   - **A** excited and proud
   - **B** sad and angry
   - **C** scared and hurt
   - **D** annoyed and frightened

6. Why do people sell lorises as pets?

   ....

   ....

   ....

Spelling

Rewrite the misspelt words.

1 The loris is <u>nocternal</u>.

....

2 It is <u>crual</u> to keep lorises as pets.

....

3 Lorises bite if they're <u>fritened</u>.

....

4 Lorises can bleed to <u>deth</u>.

....

5 Write three words from the word family that includes **fright**.

....

....

....

Vocabulary

Circle the word that has the nearest meaning to the underlined word.

6 The <u>toxin</u> deters predators.

A bite B saliva
C poison D taste

7 The toxin <u>deters</u> predators.

A discourages B provides
C persuades D annoys

8 Add a word from the text to the sentence.

Germs get into the gums and cause an

....

9 Write a word from the text to match the meaning.

a watery liquid in the mouth

....

Circle the word on each line that does **not** belong.

10 busy active energetic quiet

11 happy frightened scared fearful

Grammar

12 Complete the sentence with an adjective from the text.

It is .... to keep a slow loris as a pet.

13 Choose the correct thinking verb to complete the sentence.

I (thinking / think / thought) it is very cruel to keep slow lorises as pets.

14 Complete the sentence with an adverbial phrase from the text to tell **when**.

The loris is active ....

15 Use a connective from the box to complete the sentence correctly.

when	then	while	next	eventually

It can use both hands to eat

....

hanging upside down from a branch.

Punctuation

16 Circle the sentence that is punctuated correctly.

A It will bite if its frightened
B It will bite if it's frightened
C It will bite if it's frightened.

Rewrite each sentence correctly.

17 its very small and cute

....

....

....

18 slow lorises live in forests in asia

....

....

....

Reading and Comprehension

The turtle who wanted to fly

There was a turtle who grumbled all day long that he had no wings and couldn't fly. His friends said, 'Be satisfied the way you are. Turtles are not made to fly.' But he was not happy. Turtle grumbled so often that one day the other animals decided to teach him a lesson.

Crow said, 'Get on my back and I will take you up into the sky.' Turtle felt very proud.

When Crow had flown as high as she could, she said, 'Get on Hawk's back. He will take you higher.'

Then Hawk said, 'This is as high as I can go. Get on Eagle's back. She will take you above the clouds.'

Eagle soared above the clouds but now Turtle was frightened. He begged Eagle to take him down but Eagle just laughed. Turtle was terrified. He realised he'd been a fool to wish that he could fly. Then he remembered he had a ball of string in his pocket. He carefully tied the end of the string to Eagle's leg then dropped the ball, watching it unravel below him. Then he lowered himself safely to the ground. And he never grumbled about being stuck on the ground again.

Adapted from an American folktale

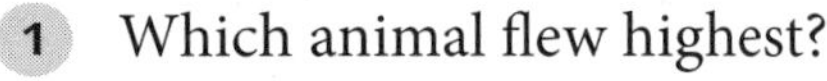

1. Which animal flew highest?
   - **A** Crow
   - **B** Eagle
   - **C** Turtle
   - **D** Hawk

2. Who said, 'Turtles are not made to fly?'
   - **A** Crow
   - **B** Turtle's friends
   - **C** all the birds
   - **D** Turtle

3. Why had Turtle been a fool?
   - **A** for complaining so much
   - **B** for trusting Eagle
   - **C** for wishing he could fly
   - **D** for grumbling

4. What happened when Turtle dropped the ball of string?
   - **A** It unravelled to the ground.
   - **B** He lost sight of it.
   - **C** It pulled Eagle's leg off.
   - **D** It landed in the clouds.

5. What did the birds hope to achieve?
   - **A** to make Turtle frightened of flying
   - **B** to show off
   - **C** to drop Turtle from the sky
   - **D** to teach Turtle a lesson

6. What is the moral of the story?

Spelling

Rewrite the misspelt words.

1 Turtle grumbeld all day long.

2 He could'nt fly.

3 The animals desided to teach him a lesson.

4 Turtle was terrafied.

5 Write three words from the word family that includes **decided**.

Vocabulary

Circle the word that has the nearest meaning to the underlined word.

6 The turtle begged for Eagle to take him to the ground.

A decided B pleaded
C asked D said

7 He realised he'd been a fool.

A hoped B understood
C noticed D remembered

8 Add a word from the text to the sentence.

Hawk said, 'This is as ______ as I can go.'

9 Write a word from the text to match the meaning.

to do something with caution and attention

Circle the word on each line that does **not** belong.

10 protested complained praised grumbled

11 frightened pleased scared terrified

Grammar

12 Complete the sentence with an adjective from the text.

At first Turtle felt ______ as he flew though the sky.

13 Choose the correct thinking verb to complete the sentence.

Turtle told the animals he (want / wanted / wanting) to fly.

14 Complete the sentence with an adverbial phrase from the text to tell **where**.

Eagle took Turtle ______.

15 Use a connective from the box to complete the sentence correctly.

When	Then	While	Next	Eventually

Turtle was safely on the ground he promised never to grumble again.

Punctuation

16 Circle the sentence that is punctuated correctly.

A Get on Hawk's back, said Crow.
B 'Get on hawks back,' said crow.
C 'Get on Hawk's back,' said Crow.

Rewrite each sentence correctly.

17 he tied the string to eagles leg

18 eagle will take you above the clouds said hawk

Reading and Comprehension

Brain food

It was Sunday. Greg was in the lounge room trying to concentrate on his homework for school the next day.

'Lunch is ready! Sit up,' called Dad from the kitchen. 'It's all brain food.'

'Ew! I don't want to eat brains,' complained Greg, walking into the kitchen.

'I am not feeding you brains. It's just food that is good for brain health. It'll help your memory and concentration.'

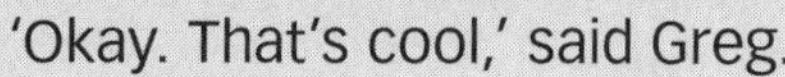

'Okay. That's cool,' said Greg.

'Look what I've made for you. Your sandwich has wholegrain bread, salmon and green spinach leaves. Then you have some strawberries and a couple of walnuts. Wacko!'

'Okay Dad. You don't have to sell it to me.'

'Well, eat that and you will power through your schoolwork. We'll add some broccoli at dinnertime and your brain will be supercharged. They're all top foods for a healthy brain and for the rest of your body too.'

1. Where does the family eat lunch?
   - **A** in the lounge room
   - **B** in the dining room
   - **C** outside
   - **D** in the kitchen
2. What was Greg doing in the lounge room?
   - **A** watching TV
   - **B** homework
   - **C** playing
   - **D** nothing
3. 'Okay. That's cool.' Why did Greg say this?
   - **A** He likes sandwiches for lunch.
   - **B** He thinks his dad is cool.
   - **C** He wants to be able to concentrate.
   - **D** He was hungry.
4. What can you infer about Dad? Choose all that apply.
   - **A** He likes to eat healthy food.
   - **B** He cares about Greg's health.
   - **C** He wants Greg to do well in school.
   - **D** He likes to eat brains.
5. Choose all that apply. How does Greg feel about lunch?
   - **A** happy to eat it
   - **B** not hungry
   - **C** not happy
   - **D** annoyed
6. Why might Dad feel he has to 'sell' Greg the lunch?

   ....

   ....

   ....

Spelling

Rewrite the misspelt words.

1 Greg was in the lownge room.

2 Greg complaned about eating brains.

3 A salmon sanwitch is healthy.

4 Brain food helps you consentrait.

5 Write three words from the word family that includes **memory**.

Vocabulary

Circle the word that has the nearest meaning to the underlined word.

6 Greg needed to finish his homework.
A acknowledge B complete
C do D accept

7 Lunch was ready.
A available B prepared
C finished D over

8 Add a word from the text to the sentence.
Sandwiches are made with slices of ________.

9 Write a word from the text to match the meaning.
a place where food is prepared

Circle the word on each line that does **not** belong.

10 promote purchase sell advertise

11 help assist hinder benefit

Grammar

12 Complete the sentence with an adjective from the text.
The sandwich had ________ spinach leaves.

13 Choose the correct thinking verb to complete the sentence.
Greg (concentrated / concentrates / concentrating) on his homework for thirty minutes.

14 Complete the sentence with an adverbial phrase from the text to tell **when**.
Dad said they'd have some broccoli ________.

15 Use a connective from the box to complete the sentence correctly.

when	then	while	next	eventually

Greg was doing his homework ________
Dad prepared lunch.

Punctuation

16 Circle the sentence that is punctuated correctly.
A 'Ew! I don't want to eat brains,' complained Greg.
B 'Ew. I don't want to eat brains' complained Greg.
C Ew! I don't want to eat brains, complained Greg.

Rewrite each sentence correctly.

17 thats cool said greg

18 lunch is ready called dad

How to make a possum nest

A ringtail possum makes its nest (called a drey) using leaves, bark, sticks and twigs. You can help possums by making a drey and hanging it in your backyard. Possums will love your sturdy and waterproof drey.

Materials

Two wire hanging baskets with liners (Note: Wire baskets are made for plants. They are very cheap to buy from a nursery or gardening shop. They come with coconut fibre liners.)

What to do

- Use one lined wire basket for the bottom of the drey.
- Take the second liner and cut an entrance hole the size of a tennis ball.
- Place the second liner upside down on top of the bottom basket.
- Wire the top and bottom together securely.
- Wrap the hanging chain around the top basket.
- Use a wire coathanger to make a hook.
- Place leaves inside to make the drey more comfortable.
- Place bark over the top for added protection from the rain.

1 The liner is made of

- **A** coconut fibre.
- **B** wire.
- **C** a hanging basket.
- **D** leaves, bark, twigs and sticks.

2 What lives in a drey?

- **A** birds
- **B** koalas
- **C** plants
- **D** ringtail possums

3 What size is a ringtail possum?

- **A** the size of a cat
- **B** as big as a hanging basket
- **C** the size of a tennis ball
- **D** smaller than a koala

4 Why do you need a hook?

- **A** to hook the top and bottom parts together
- **B** to make the drey sturdy
- **C** to use a wire coathanger
- **D** to hang the drey from a tree

5 Choose all that apply. Make the drey comfortable

- **A** so that birds like it too.
- **B** so that possums move in.
- **C** to be kind to animals.
- **D** because possums live in nests.

6 How does this drey help possums?

....

....

....

Spelling

Rewrite the misspelt words.

1 Hanging baskets are cheep to purchase.

....

2 Wire the top and bottom together securly.

....

3 Give the drey pretection from the rain.

....

4 Purchase baskets from a nursury.

....

5 Write three words from the word family that includes **secure**.

....

....

....

Vocabulary

Circle the word that has the nearest meaning to the underlined word.

6 Wire the top and bottom together securely.

A firmly B quickly
C loosely D evenly

7 Make the drey more comfortable.

A happy B cool
C warm D cosy

8 Add a word from the text to the sentence.

Most birds lay their eggs in a

....

9 Write a word from the text to match the meaning.

a nest for a ringtail possum

....

Circle the word on each line that does **not** belong.

10 safety discomfort shelter protection

11 cheap pricey inexpensive economical

Grammar

12 Complete the sentence with an adjective from the text.

Make the drey .... for the possum.

13 Choose the correct thinking verb to complete the sentence.

Mum has always (loving / loves / loved) possums.

14 Complete the sentence with an adverbial phrase from the text to tell **where**.

Wrap the chain ....

15 Use a connective from the box to complete the sentence correctly.

When	Then	While	Next	Eventually

Hang the drey in your backyard.

....

a possum might move in.

Punctuation

16 Circle the sentence that is punctuated correctly.

A 'Let's build a possum nest,' suggested Mum.

B 'Let's build a possum nest' suggested Mum

C 'Let's build a possum nest? suggested Mum.'

Rewrite each sentence correctly.

17 the nest is constructed with leaves bark sticks and twigs

....

....

18 a possum nest is called a drey

....

....

Reading and Comprehension

Write a common noun from the box in each space.

attention	fun	activities	meat	plastic
day	people	trees	life	earth

1 Earth Day is a special ____________. Earth Day focuses people's ____________ on caring for the ____________.

2 Earth Day ____________ include planting ____________, refusing to buy ____________ and eating less ____________.

3 In real ____________ breakfast cereal doesn't make ____________ have more ____________.

Write a common noun from the box in each space.

ground	trees	sky	website	string	day	cage	lesson	service	night

4 A bird in a ____________ will never soar through the ____________.

5 Slow lorises sleep in the ____________ all ____________ and are active at ____________.

6 'Lost and Found Pets' is a ____________ that provides a community ____________.

7 Turtle used ____________ to get back to the ____________. The birds taught Turtle a ____________.

Spelling

The spelling mistakes in these sentences have been circled. Write the correct spelling on the lines.

8 (Recycal) everything you can. ____________

9 Earth Day is a (spechal) day. ____________

10 Some TV ads have good (musik). ____________

11 A set of two things is a (pear). ____________

12 The cat went missing on (Wensday). ____________

13 I (coodent) find my school hat. ____________

14 The turtle was (terafied) of flying. ____________

15 It's important to eat (helthy) foods. ____________

Answers

Unit 1A page 8

1. B. See lines 14–15.
2. C. See lines 4–5.
3. D. You can infer that Mum makes this statement because she responds to the narrator's previous statement to her.
4. C. You can infer that Dani cares more about her brain than her hair because she does wear a helmet.
5. D. You can judge that the narrator thinks Dani is smart because she knows that wearing a helmet will protect her brain.
6. You can judge that the narrator thinks helmets are important. The narrator says that it's stupid not to wear a helmet.

Unit 1B page 9

1. wear
2. friends
3. safety
4. sensible
5. helmets, worries
6. B.
7. C.
8. protect
9. helmet
10. stupid
11. safety
12. brain
13. Wear
14. at the dining table
15. or
16. B.
17. Dani needs her brain.
18. 'I always wear a helmet,' said Dani.

Unit 2A page 10

1. C.
2. D.
3. B, C. You can infer that gorillas are endangered because people are destroying their habitat and killing them to eat (bushmeat) or for trade in gorilla parts. Leopards might kill a number of baby gorillas but this is natural and would not happen frequently enough to make the species endangered.
4. C. You can infer that the silverback protects the troop.
5. D. You can judge that the silverback is the boss of the troop. Others look up to him.
6. You can judge that gorillas are sociable. They communicate with each other. They live in a troop to help and support each other. They mourn when one of the troop dies.

Unit 2B page 11

1. communicate
2. herbivores
3. species
4. bushmeat
5. gorillas, babies
6. B.
7. C.
8. attacked
9. foliage
10. attack
11. forest
12. adults
13. eat
14. in Africa/in forests/in social groups
15. or/and
16. C.
17. Gorillas bark if there's danger.
18. A baby drinks its mother's milk.

Unit 3A page 12

1. C. See line 11.
2. B. See line 15.
3. B. You can infer that Lizard hid because he knew Galah would be angry with him.
4. A. You can infer that the spikes were thorns or prickles from the bindeah bush.
5. A. You can judge that the accident happened because 'Lizard started to show off for the galah, throwing the boomerang harder and harder'.
6. You can judge that Lizard deserved to be punished for showing off. His punishment is fair because it matches the bald patch that Galah has. You might also judge that Galah was unfair. Lizard had not meant to harm Galah.

Unit 3B page 13

1. watched
2. proud
3. bleeding
4. bald
5. throwing, shrieked/shrieking
6. B.
7. D.
8. grabbed
9. boomerang
10. happiness
11. whispered
12. lizard
13. threw
14. through the air
15. and
16. B.
17. Galah shrieked and screamed.
18. Galah said, 'You shall be covered in spikes.'

Answers

Unit 4A page 14

1. B. See lines 10–11.
2. B. See line 10.
3. D. You can infer that rabbits came to Australia by ship because they arrived on the First Fleet.
4. C. You can infer that the hare is the judge.
5. A, B. You can judge that it is not a good idea to promote rabbits as wonderful for Australia because they are a feral pest and they compete with native animals for food.
6. You can judge that when you buy chocolate bilbies you can support projects to save wild bilbies.

Unit 4B page 15

1. whether
2. should
3. easily
4. careful
5. bilbies, donating
6. A.
7. C.
8. chocolate
9. pest
10. survival
11. minor
12. projects
13. breed
14. in Australia
15. they
16. C.
17. The Easter bunny idea comes from German folklore.
18. European rabbits came to Australia on the First Fleet.

Unit 5A page 16

1. B. See line 9.
2. B. See the photo.
3. A, B, C, D. You can infer that the recipe is easy to make for all the reasons listed.
4. B. You can infer that the mixture is too thick if the ingredients won't combine.
5. A or B or C. You can judge whether the recipe is child friendly or not, based on your own experiences.
6. You can judge that dates and orange juice make the balls sweet.

Unit 5B page 17

1. amount
2. healthy
3. dairy
4. juice
5. allergies, processing/ processes
6. D.
7. C.
8. treat
9. zest
10. add
11. bitter
12. treat
13. Add
14. in extra coconut
15. I
16. B.
17. Linda said, 'I like coconut.'
18. Paul made a tasty snack.

Unit 6A page 18

1. D. See line 4.
2. C. See line 17.
3. B. You can infer that Mum cares for the environment and likes to have fun.
4. A, B, C. You can infer that swimmers could be safe from wild surf, sharks, boats and surf craft.
5. D. You can judge that the outing is extremely important to the family.
6. You can judge from the clues in the text that the family is friendly, fit and active, sociable and they care for the environment.

Unit 6B page 19

1. family
2. Sometimes
3. beach
4. favourite
5. reminding, families
6. D.
7. B.
8. friends
9. shade
10. protected
11. spoilt
12. area
13. play
14. on the council barbecue
15. it
16. C.
17. Mum said, 'Pick up the rubbish.'
18. There's no surf so it's very safe.

Unit 7A page 20

1. D. See lines 2, 10.
2. B. See lines 3–5.
3. A. You can infer that Dad and the poet cycle.
4. D. You can infer that on a footpath bikes, dogs and people can be dangerous.
5. D. You can judge that Grandma is the most considerate person. She tells readers how she follows the rules for sharing with everyone.
6. You can judge that cycling is healthy and fun or that it is a bit scary if people don't follow the rules or aren't considerate. You can agree or disagree with comments in the poem about footpath use.

Answers

Unit 7B page 21

1. rules
2. bicycle
3. dangerous
4. people
5. saying, cycled/cycling
6. D.
7. B.
8. cycling/walking
9. considerate
10. humour
11. assist
12. Drivers
13. Share
14. on the road/on the footpath
15. she
16. A.
17. 'I love cycling,' said Dad.
18. Grandma says, 'Stick to the left.'

Revision 1 pages 22–23

1. brain, important, bicycle, skateboard
2. gorilla, leopard, silverback, troop
3. bilbies, bunnies
4. zest, orange
5. dairy, eggs, nuts
6. equipment, shade, rubbish
7. rules, safety
8. friends
9. safety
10. communicate
11. herbivores
12. proud
13. careful
14. healthy
15. favourite
16. weather
17. safety
18. nests
19. eat
20. in Australia
21. it
22. so
23. David said, 'I love the beach.'
24. The Easter bunny idea comes from German folklore.
25. Grandma said, 'Share the footpath.'

NAPLAN-style Reading Test 1 page 24

1. B. See lines 11–12.
2. C. See lines 7–8.
3. B. You can infer that the cat checked supplies once a month.
4. B, C (and maybe also A). You can judge that the rat betrayed the king and the cat. You might also judge that the king betrayed the cat by dismissing her from her job.
5. B, C. You can judge that the cat was angry that she had lost her job and wanted to punish the rat.
6. B, D. You can judge that the girl lost her job because she would have known or should have guessed that the rat was stealing the king's goods for her. She did not report the crime to the cat or the king so the king thought she deserved to lose her job.
7. A, B, D. You might judge that the king was mean for dismissing the cat and that the cat should not have been punished at all, and that the rat was a fool.
   OR
   C, D. You might judge that the cat deserved to be punished and that the rat was a fool.

NAPLAN-style Language Conventions Test 1 page 25

1. steal
2. punished
3. thief
4. worked
5. B.
6. C.
7. C.
8. C.
9. D.
10. B.
11. B.
12. C.

Unit 8A page 26

1. B. See line 4.
2. A. See line 5.
3. D. You can infer that walking or cycling saves energy and saving energy helps the earth.
4. B. You can infer that refilling a water bottle is better for the earth than throwing out a disposable plastic bottle.
5. A, B, C, D. You can judge that all answers are correct.
6. You can judge that there needs to be a specific Earth Day to focus people's attention on caring for the earth.

Unit 8B page 27

1. Twenty
2. recycle
3. Use
4. special
5. refillable, uncaring
6. A.
7. C.
8. reduce
9. volunteering
10. observe
11. neglect
12. special
13. focuses

Answers

14. in 1970
15. Next
16. A.
17. Lots of celebrities support Earth Day.
18. Earth Day and Anzac Day are both special.

Unit 9A page 28

1. B. See lines 3–4.
2. A, B, C, D. See lines 11–13, 17.
3. B. You can infer that the writer saw and heard the ad on television.
4. C. You can infer that the writer liked the music most. She noticed the music first and that it was 'good'. Nothing else in the ad is described as good.
5. D. You can judge from the writer's comments that she thought the ad was totally untruthful.
6. You should judge that some people will buy the cereal because they don't read boxes to notice the 28% sugar; they might believe what the advertisers claim; or they like the taste of this type of cereal.

Unit 9B page 29

1. music
2. breakfast
3. laughing
4. reasons
5. unhealthy, misleading
6. A.
7. D.
8. supermarket/box
9. cereal
10. honest
11. depressed
12. misleading
13. know
14. After breakfast
15. then
16. C.
17. Breakfast cereal doesn't make people happy.
18. The children were laughing, smiling and playing.

Unit 10A page 30

1. D. See lines 13–15.
2. C. See lines 8–12.
3. A. You can infer that the bird lives alone.
4. C. You can infer that the bird was born to 'fly, nest in a tree and find a mate'.
5. A, C, D. You can judge that the bird is sad, bored and lonely. The bird describes wanting to be a pair. The bird longs to soar through the sky. The bird says all it has is time so you can infer it is bored with nothing to do to fill its time.
6. You can judge that the bird wishes for the impossible—to be free. It's impossible because a caged bird, born in captivity, would not survive in the wild if it was set free.

Unit 10B page 31

1. through
2. heart
3. stretching
4. pair
5. undo/redo, impossible
6. C.
7. C.
8. bars
9. wings
10. beak
11. baby
12. feathered
13. wish
14. through bars
15. while
16. A.
17. 'What am I?' asked the bird.
18. The bird couldn't fly.

Unit 11A page 32

1. C. See lines 18–19.
2. B. See lines 15–16.
3. C. You can infer that the purpose of the site is to report missing and found pets.
4. D. You can infer that a community organisation is a group that helps people living in the community.
5. A. You can judge that Doug is a caring person because he writes the notice on behalf of Chorizo's owner. The owner is 'distraught' and Doug wants to help her.
6. You can judge that the website would be very useful for people who have lost a pet or for people who have found one and need to contact the owner.

Unit 11B page 33

1. hungry
2. wriggled
3. Wednesday
4. chased
5. wandering, wanders, wanderer, wandered
6. C.
7. B.
8. service
9. leash
10. hide
11. despised
12. nasty
13. think
14. at around 1:30 am
15. Eventually/Then
16. C.
17. I'm at Rainbow Beach.
18. Amy lost her budgie in Sorrento.

Answers

Unit 12A page 34

1. A. See line 11.
2. C. See line 3.
3. C. You can infer that Molly wants people to know not to buy wild animals such as the slow loris as pets.
4. C. You can infer that poachers in this text are people who steal animals from the wild.
5. B. You can judge that Molly feels sad for the lorises and angry that this happens to them.
6. You can judge that the people who sell the lorises do so to make money. You can judge that the slow loris is easy to catch and small to carry and keep in a cage. Poachers can only sell lorises if people want to buy them. You can judge that some people want to buy cute or unusual pets.

Unit 12B page 35

1. nocturnal
2. cruel
3. frightened
4. death
5. frightened, frightens, frightening, frightful
6. C.
7. A.
8. infection
9. saliva
10. quiet
11. happy
12. cruel
13. think
14. at night
15. while
16. C.
17. It's very small and cute.
18. Slow lorises live in forests in Asia.

Unit 13A page 36

1. B. See lines 12–13.
2. B. See lines 3–4.
3. C. You can infer that Turtle had been a fool to wish he could fly.
4. A. You can infer that the string unravelled to the ground.
5. D. You can judge that the birds wanted to teach Turtle a lesson because they were tired of his grumbling.
6. You can judge that the moral of the story is: be satisfied with who you are and don't wish to be something that you are not.

Unit 13B page 37

1. grumbled
2. couldn't
3. decided
4. terrified
5. decide, deciding, decision, decisive, decided, undecided
6. B.
7. B.
8. high
9. carefully
10. praised
11. pleased
12. proud
13. wanted
14. above the clouds
15. When
16. C.
17. He tied the string to Eagle's leg.
18. 'Eagle will take you above the clouds,' said Hawk.

Unit 14A page 38

1. D. See lines 6–8.
2. B. See lines 2–4.
3. C. You can infer that Greg thinks food to help him concentrate is 'cool'.
4. A, B, C. You can infer that Dad likes to eat healthy food and that he gives Greg healthy food because he cares about Greg's health and wants him to do well at school.
5. A. You can judge that Greg is happy to eat the lunch because he tells Dad, 'You don't have to sell it to me.'
6. You can judge that Dad might have felt he needed to 'sell' the lunch because some of the foods might not have been very popular with Greg.

Unit 14B page 39

1. lounge
2. complained
3. sandwich
4. concentrate
5. memorise, memories, memorising, memorised, remember, remembering, remembered, remembers
6. B.
7. B.
8. bread
9. kitchen
10. purchase
11. hinder
12. green
13. concentrated
14. at dinnertime
15. while
16. A.
17. 'That's cool,' said Greg.
18. 'Lunch is ready!' called Dad.

Answers

Unit 15A page 40

1. A. See line 11.
2. D. See line 2.
3. C. You can infer that the possum must be the same size as the entrance—the size of a tennis ball.
4. D. You can infer that a hook will be needed to hang the drey in the backyard.
5. B. You can judge that the best way to encourage possums to move in is to make the drey comfortable.
6. You can judge that this drey will help possums because it gives them a sturdy and comfortable ready-made home and it will help to protect them from rain, cold and cats.

Unit 15B page 41

1. cheap
2. securely
3. protection
4. nursery
5. secures, secured, securely, security, securing, insecure, insecurity
6. A.
7. D.
8. nest
9. drey
10. discomfort
11. pricey
12. comfortable
13. loved
14. around the top basket
15. Eventually/Then
16. A.
17. The nest is constructed with leaves, bark, sticks and twigs.
18. A possum nest is called a drey.

Revision 2 pages 42–43

1. day, attention, earth
2. activities, trees, plastic, meat
3. life, people, fun
4. cage, sky
5. trees, day, night
6. website, service
7. string, ground, lesson
8. Recycle
9. special
10. music
11. pair
12. Wednesday
13. couldn't
14. terrified
15. healthy
16. cheap
17. uncomfortable
18. terrified
19. taught
20. on the ground
21. he
22. because
23. 'Take me back down,' said the turtle.
24. The turtle couldn't fly.
25. A crow, a hawk and an eagle took a turtle into the sky.

NAPLAN-style Reading Test 2 page 44

1. C. See line 13.
2. C. See lines 3–4.
3. B. You can infer that Baxter is Ava's dog. Baxter is concerned about Ava throughout the text.
4. B. You can infer that Baxter is taken for a walk after school.
5. B. You can judge that Ava is not frightened. If she was concerned at all she would let Baxter out to protect her.
6. D. You can judge that Baxter is very protective of Ava. He was not happy to hear angry voices. He was desperate to get out through the gate to protect Ava.
7. C. You can judge that Baxter snarls to show anger.

NAPLAN-style Language Conventions Test 2 page 45

1. heard
2. whimpered
3. growling
4. wasn't
5. B.
6. D.
7. C.
8. A.
9. B.
10. D.
11. D.
12. A.

Unit 16A page 46

1. B. See lines 17–18.
2. B. See lines 4–5.
3. D. You can infer that, in this text, poaching means to kill gorillas for their meat or parts.
4. A, B, C, D. You can infer that all the answers are correct.
5. A, B, D. You can judge that illegal mining takes place because coltan is valuable for use in mobile phones. People break the law to get it to sell. Illegal mining is bad for the environment as well as for farmers trying to work their land.
6. You can judge that recycling mobile phones, so that the coltan is reused, prevents the destruction of natural areas to mine more coltan.

Answers

Unit 16B page 47

1. illegal
2. losing
3. mobile
4. habitat
5. threats, threatened, threatening, threaten
6. A.
7. B.
8. garbage
9. mining
10. cheap
11. hinder
12. your old mobile phones
13. is
14. happily
15. Unless
16. C.
17. Farmers with no income sell gorilla meat.
18. The organisation is called Gorilla Doctors.

Unit 17A page 48

1. D. See lines 2–5.
2. B. See lines 8–13.
3. A. You can infer that Arthur got carried away with the story and spoke to the characters.
4. A. You can infer that Banjo must be their dog.
5. B. You can judge that Arthur is excited about the story and interested in the events in the children's lives.
6. C. You can judge that Arthur is reading an adventure story.

Unit 17B page 49

1. light
2. comfortable
3. uncle
4. clothes
5. quickly, quicker, quickest, quicken
6. A.
7. C.
8. cool
9. library
10. pushing
11. murmur
12. the
13. was
14. loudly
15. When
16. B.
17. 'Quickly,' he said.
18. Arthur read a library book.

Unit 18A page 50

1. B. See line 2.
2. C. See line 17.
3. A. You can infer that birds become stronger and healthier in the rehabilitation centre.
4. A. You can infer that an infrared camera helped Nana see the owl in the dark.
5. D. You can judge that the owl needed to be returned to the same area where it was found as this was its natural territory.
6. You can judge that Nana feels useful, happy and proud to be a volunteer.

Unit 18B page 51

1. volunteers
2. nowhere
3. released
4. rehabilitation
5. injure, injury, injuries, injuring, uninjured
6. C.
7. A.
8. rehabilitation
9. aviary
10. agreed
11. caged
12. the wild bird rehabilitation centre
13. is
14. quickly
15. unless
16. B.
17. Nana's group cares for injured birds.
18. The little owl couldn't fly.

Unit 19A page 52

1. D. See lines 12–13.
2. B. See lines 18–19.
3. A, C, D. You can infer that farming tools make work easier. The tools might cost too much for poor farmers or they might not be available in remote areas.
4. A. You can infer that farmers want and need a fair payment for their produce.
5. A, B. You can judge that Fairtrade helps workers and farmers get fair wages and better working conditions. It also helps ensure there are doctors and schools available for the villagers.
6. You can judge that Fairtrade is important to help farmers/producers. You can judge that without organisations such as Fairtrade, people might not get fair wages; workers might be mistreated; crops might not grow as well; farmers could be very poor.

Answers

Unit 19B page 53

1. chocolate
2. countries
3. taught
4. environment
5. protecting, protection, protected, protects, unprotected
6. B.
7. B.
8. symbol
9. tools
10. improve
11. dust
12. a
13. are
14. fairly
15. As well as
16. A.
17. Farmers in Papua New Guinea grow cocoa.
18. Fairtrade ANZ works in Samoa.

Unit 20A page 54

1. D. See line 2.
2. C. See line 14.
3. C. You can infer that Odelia is returning to school.
4. D. You can infer that they planted taro in case the borers destroyed all the cocoa pods. Odelia's mother would need to grow something to sell if her cocoa trees failed.
5. B. You can judge that Odelia had missed school to help her mother save their farm.
6. You might judge that you would not like to live Odelia's life because she works hard on the farm. You might also judge that it would be good to live on a farm.

Unit 20B page 55

1. quickly
2. troubles
3. worried
4. diseased
5. excite, exciting, excitement, excites, unexcited, excitable, unexciting
6. C.
7. B.
8. absent
9. pest
10. worried
11. helping
12. The Fairtrade people
13. was
14. quickly
15. then
16. A.
17. Odelia's mother is a farmer.
18. Odelia lives in Papua New Guinea.

Unit 21A page 56

1. C. See lines 20–21.
2. A. See line 13.
3. D. You can infer that councils support the project because they assist with funding or by providing schools with the right trees for their area.
4. C. You can infer that more trees will be planted this way.
5. C. You can judge that making oxygen is the most important thing trees do.
6. You could judge that the project is worthwhile because of the reasons given in the text and because it is important for as many schools as possible to get involved. You could judge that your school is already involved in other projects.

Unit 21B page 57

1. world
2. activity
3. communities
4. numerous
5. govern, governs, governing, governed
6. B.
7. C.
8. benefits
9. benefits
10. preventing
11. taking
12. The project
13. are
14. proudly
15. therefore
16. C.
17. The project was launched by Olivia Newton-John and Jon Dee.
18. 'It's a tremendous project,' said the teacher.

Unit 22A page 58

1. C. See lines 2 and 7.
2. D. See line 11.
3. B. You can infer that it damages the silk and that damaged silk is less valuable.
4. B. You can infer that the worm stage is the longest. This is the only stage where the silkworm eats. It does not eat as a pupa or moth.
5. A, B or D. You could judge:
   A. It's a short life but they eat their favourite food all the time so it's sweet.
   OR
   B. It's sad because they are killed for their silk and they don't have a chance to find a mate.
   OR
   D. They are busy most of their lives eating and then making silk and transforming into moths

but they spend their lives alone.

6. You could judge that they think it is cruel to boil the pupa alive.

Unit 22B page 59

1. moult
2. cocoons
3. dissolve
4. hole
5. allow, allowing, allows, allowance, allowances, disallowed
6. B.
7. C.
8. transform
9. enzymes
10. disappears
11. dies
12. The silk thread
13. was
14. naturally
15. then
16. A.
17. The silkworm's cocoon is made of silk.
18. 'My silkworms have hatched,' said Oliver.

Unit 23A page 60

1. B. See lines 4–5.
2. A. See line 7.
3. B. You can infer Mum trusted them with the decision about which dog to choose.
4. B. You can infer that the dog was called Panda because it had black and white fur.
5. A, D. You can judge that an energetic dog needs an energetic owner and a person allergic to cats should not have a cat.
6. You can judge that in order to find the right match you need to consider your personality, your situation and your budget then ask animal shelter staff to suggest suitable matches for you.

Unit 23B page 61

1. decided
2. useful
3. particular
4. Choosing
5. suits, suitable, suitability, suited, suitably
6. A.
7. B.
8. treated
9. shelter
10. correct
11. problem
12. Mum, Paul and I
13. have been/are
14. carefully
15. as well as
16. C.
17. We decided we'd adopt a pet.
18. Mum said, 'I trust you to choose.'

Revision 3 pages 62–63

1. phones, gorillas, school, money, Doctors
2. owl, moths
3. coffee, tea, chocolate
4. hatch, eat, grow, spin, transform
5. adopt, choose
6. make, store
7. give
8. mobile
9. habitat
10. illegal
11. countries
12. environment
13. communities
14. comfortable
15. cycle
16. hole
17. dislike
18. cocoons
19. provide/give/are
20. quickly/quietly/carefully
21. they
22. therefore/so
23. 'It's time for reading,' said the teacher.
24. 'Is that a good book?' asked the teacher.
25. Cocoa is grown in Papua New Guinea.

NAPLAN-style Reading Test 3 page 64

1. D. See line 5.
2. A. See lines 16–17.
3. A. You can infer that Rama knew to stand her ground. She'd learned from past experience. She'd seen what had happened to a friend.
4. B and C. You can infer that Rama's attitude confused the dragon. She did not show fear. Nor did she turn and run away.
5. C. You can infer that Rama had been holding her breath the whole time the dragon was summing her up. She could relax and breathe once the dragon turned back into the cave.
6. D. You can judge that this is part of a fantasy adventure story.
7. You can judge whether or not this story character interests you and if you would like to find out what happens to her. Justify your answer with reasons.

NAPLAN-style Language Conventions Test 3 page 65

1. claws
2. fearsome
3. breathing

4. powerful
5. D.
6. B.
7. C.
8. B.
9. C.
10. B.
11. A.
12. B.

Unit 24A page 66

1. A. See line 19.
2. C. See lines 15–16.
3. B. You can infer that Jack had arrived at 6:30 because it would be two hours before playground supervision commenced at 8:30 am.
4. B. You can infer that he had a drink and gave up the idea of looking for lost coins.
5. A. You can judge that Jack had grown out of his school jumper but that his family could not afford to buy him a new one.
6. D. You can judge that Eric is thoughtful and dependable because he regularly brings food to share with Jack. Jack also seems hopeful that Eric might bring a spare jumper for him.

Unit 24B page 67

1. arrived
2. building
3. weren't
4. stomach
5. supervise, supervised, supervising, supervises, unsupervised
6. B.
7. B.
8. money
9. lucky
10. ended
11. stolen
12. His stomach
13. commented
14. outside the locked toilet block
15. consequently
16. C.
17. He'd wait for Eric.
18. 'Hello Eric,' said Jack.

Unit 25A page 68

1. C. See lines 12–13.
2. C. See lines 4–6.
3. B. You can infer that the centre is designed specifically for swimming.
4. D. You can infer that the physiotherapist works with people who have injuries.
5. C. You can judge that consultation means that lots of people were asked for ideas and suggestions.
6. You can judge that people who work 5 am to 9 pm all year round could never use the centre.

Unit 25B page 69

1. National
2. suitable
3. vegetable
4. energetic
5. disability, disabled, disabling, able, ability, abilities, unable
6. C.
7. B.
8. open
9. construction
10. awful
11. disadvantage
12. Their smoothies and vegetable juices/Their healthy foods and beverages
13. praised
14. on Saturday
15. consequently
16. A.
17. 'The pool is amazing,' said Felicity.
18. Sofie Ray has joined the swim squad.

Unit 26A page 70

1. C. See line 16.
2. B. See lines 10–11.
3. C. You can infer that the photo is of Jonathan.
4. A, B, D. You can infer that Louise Sauvage is an Australian track and field champion who has a disability.
5. C. You can judge that Jonathan is a happy boy with a positive attitude.
6. D. You can judge that Jonathan's parents would be proud of him and his attitude because he is prepared to try his hardest to achieve his goals.

Unit 26B page 71

1. champion
2. successful
3. disability
4. internationally
5. compete, competition, competitive, competes, competed, competitively, uncompetitive
6. C.
7. C.
8. hero
9. control
10. surrender
11. weakness
12. my sporting hero/a sporting hero/a role model for all Australians
13. tells
14. with a disability
15. Alternatively
16. B.

Answers

17. 'Louise Sauvage is my hero,' said Jonathan.
18. They've got the same motto.

Unit 27A page 72

1. B. See line 5.
2. B. See lines 15–16.
3. A, B, C, D. You can infer that submerged objects are dangerous for each suggested reason.
4. A, C, D. You can infer that the only thing a dead animal couldn't do is bite you.
5. B, C. You can infer that the ad was successful because it caught Fatima's attention, she remembered what it was about and it made her think.
6. You can judge that floodwater can arrive suddenly, move quickly and be very powerful.

Unit 27B page 73

1. dangerous
2. persuade
3. caught
4. submerged
5. waters, watery, watered, watering, waterfall
6. B.
7. D.
8. submerged
9. reporter
10. dangerous
11. calming
12. their car
13. sweep
14. into floodwater
15. alternatively
16. B.
17. Sometimes floodwater doesn't look dangerous.
18. Fatima's review was interesting.

Unit 28A page 74

1. B. See line 4.
2. D. See lines 16–17.
3. B. You can infer that a gold coin donation means at least one dollar.
4. D. You can infer that above all else Kelsey has developed confidence in herself.
5. D. You can judge that Justin is proud of his sister and pleased that she loves dancing.
6. D. You can judge that the best thing about dancing is seeing Kelsey having fun.

Unit 28B page 75

1. rhythm
2. coordination
3. community
4. confidence
5. celebrate, celebrated, celebrations, celebrity, celebrities
6. D.
7. C.
8. balance
9. confidence
10. talent
11. group
12. her head
13. are
14. in dancing classes
15. also
16. A.
17. 'I love dancing!' declared Kelsey. / 'I love dancing,' declared Kelsey.
18. 'You're a great dancer!' said Mum. / 'You're a great dancer,' said Mum.

Unit 29A page 76

1. B. See line 17.
2. A. See lines 12–13.
3. A. You can infer that Mum has been working on a time machine.
4. D. You can infer that Mum has disappeared in time, into the future.
5. A, B, D. You can judge that Mum is obsessed with work because the children rarely see her. You can infer that she is smart because she is a scientist. You can infer that she is secretive because she has worked on the machine for months and not told the children about it.
6. You can judge that the children would like to fiddle with the computer or try out the machine. Perhaps they might try to find their mother. Perhaps they might report to their father.

Unit 29B page 77

1. garage
2. Curiosity
3. windscreen
4. machine
5. obedient, obey, obeying, obeyed, obeys, disobedient, disobeys, disobeying, disobeyed
6. D.
7. C.
8. hovered
9. weird
10. skill
11. indifferent
12. Their mum
13. were
14. above a spinning base
15. consequently

16. C.
17. Mum was a scientist and she'd had a breakthrough.
18. 'What's happened?' asked Noomi.

Unit 30A page 78

1. D. See line 3.
2. B. See line 4.
3. C. You can infer that her role was to entertain through giving people rides.
4. C. You can infer that Sigrid thinks the book helps people understand the life of a zoo animal.
5. C. You can judge that Sigrid believed Queenie was treated unfairly.
6. You can judge that modern laws are kinder to animals than laws in the past were. You can judge that this is in the best interest of the animals.

Unit 30B page 79

1. elephant
2. captured
3. recommend
4. accidentally
5. destroys, destroyed, destroying, destruction, indestructible
6. D.
7. B.
8. illustrator
9. crowds
10. wild
11. returned
12. her herd/a family
13. lives
14. from the wild/from her family
15. she
16. B.
17. Queenie lived in a zoo in Melbourne.
18. 'Think about captive animals,' said Sigrid.

Revision 4 pages 80–81

1. athlete, medals, Australia
2. herds, wild, zoos, animals, hunters
3. balance, coordination
4. dangerous, swiftly, submerged, animals, flooded
5. foods, juices, energetic
6. disabilities
7. machine
8. arrived
9. suitable
10. vegetable
11. persuade
12. community
13. celebration
14. garage
15. machine
16. through
17. result
18. athlete/champion
19. compete
20. at the swimming pool/at the swim centre/in the pool
21. they
22. or
23. 'Great dancing, Keith,' called Nicole.
24. 'What's happened to Mum?' asked Noomi.
25. 'That's a great story,' said Darcey.

NAPLAN-style Reading Test 4 page 82

1. C. See line 2.
2. B. See line 3.
3. C. You can infer that Isaac would have thought of his mother's health and safety first.
4. C. You can infer that the burglars were looking for money.
5. B. You can judge that they are friends. They walk home from school together and live in the same street.
6. A. You can infer that the burglars were looking for valuables hidden in the fridge.
7. D. You can judge that Isaac was embarrassed because Scarlet could see his underpants on the floor.

NAPLAN-style Language Conventions Test 4 page 83

1. burst
2. soccer
3. scattered
4. valuables
5. A.
6. B.
7. C.
8. D.
9. B.
10. C.
11. C.
12. B.

Vocabulary

16 Circle the correct word in the brackets.
Hanging baskets are (cheap / cheep) to purchase.

17 Circle the word that means the opposite of **comfortable**.
cosy pleasant uncomfortable comforting

Grammar

18 Add an adjective to the sentence.
A ____________________ turtle did not want to fly so high.

19 Add a verb to the sentence.
The birds ____________________ turtle a lesson.

20 Add an adverbial phrase to tell **where**.
Turtles are meant to stay ____________________.

21 Add a pronoun to the sentence.
The turtle decided ____________________ would never complain again.

22 Add a connective to the sentence.
Turtle was not made to fly ____________________ he has no wings.

Punctuation

Rewrite each sentence correctly.

23 Take me back down said the turtle

____

____

24 the turtle couldnt fly

____

____

25 a crow a hawk and an eagle took a turtle into the sky

____

____

Trouble on Smith Street

Baxter heard voices and rushed to the fence. He saw Ava and her brother Tim coming home from school. They were late. He saw other children following them. He didn't know the others. He barked to say hello to Ava, and wagged his tail. He'd have his afternoon walk now. Then he heard angry shouting. He was confused. Why didn't Ava open the gate and come into the yard? It would be dark in a little while. He peered through the wire fence. He barked again then whimpered and scratched at the bottom of the gate.

The voices were angry. Something wasn't right. Baxter wasn't happy. He stuck his head through the gap in the gate. He saw Ava arguing with another child. Baxter snarled. He wanted Ava to open the gate and let him out.

'Let me out,' he called. He rushed up and down the fence, nose to the ground, growling and snarling loudly, 'Ava, I'm here.'

All the while the loud, angry voices continued outside the fence.

1 Why was Baxter unhappy?

- **A** His head got stuck in the fence.
- **B** Ava didn't say hello.
- **C** He knew something wasn't right.
- **D** He'd been alone all day.

2 Where had Ava and Tim been?

- **A** inside the house
- **B** outside the gate
- **C** at school
- **D** out playing

3 Whose dog is it?

- **A** Baxter's
- **B** Ava's
- **C** Tim's
- **D** Ava's neighbour's

4 What usually happens after school?

- **A** Ava and Tim play with other children.
- **B** Ava takes Baxter for a walk.
- **C** Ava and Tim argue with other children.
- **D** Ava and Tim play with Baxter.

5 Do you think Ava is frightened?

- **A** No. Ava is arguing so she mustn't be frightened.
- **B** No. If Ava was frightened she'd let Baxter out.
- **C** Yes because she is ignoring Baxter.
- **D** Yes because she is shouting and arguing.

6 How does Baxter feel about Ava?

- **A** angry
- **B** dangerous
- **C** very vicious
- **D** very protective

7 How does Baxter show anger?

- **A** He barks.
- **B** He whimpers.
- **C** He snarls.
- **D** He calls, 'Let me out.'

NAPLAN-STYLE 2 CONVENTIONS OF LANGUAGE TEST

Spelling

The spelling mistakes in these sentences have been underlined. Write the correct spelling on the lines.

1. Baxter herd children shouting. ______________________

2. Baxter wimpered. ______________________

3. Baxter was growlling loudly. ______________________

4. Something was'nt right. ______________________

Vocabulary

5. Which word means **puzzled**?

   A worried B confused C annoyed D angry

6. Which word does **not** belong?

   A whimpering B whining C crying D barking

7. Which word does **not** belong?

   A correct B right C unfair D appropriate

Grammar

8. Which adjective describes the children's voices?

   A angry B quiet C peaceful D happy

9. Which word is a thinking verb?
   Baxter wanted Ava to open the gate.

   A Baxter B wanted C open D the gate

10. Which adverbial phrase tells when it would be dark?

    A through the wire fence B outside the fence

    C into the year D in a little while

Punctuation

11. Which sentence is punctuated correctly?

    A 'Let me out' he called. B 'Let me out he called.'

    C Let me out, he called. D 'Let me out,' he called.

12. Which sentence is punctuated correctly?

    A Baxter wasn't happy. B Baxter wasnt happy.

    C Baxter was'nt happy. D Baxter wasn't happy

UNIT 16A

Reading and Comprehension

Our school is calling on you

Raise money for endangered gorillas.

GIVE US YOUR OLD MOBILE PHONES.

Our school supports the work of the Gorilla Doctors—vets in Rwanda, Uganda and the Democratic Republic of Congo (DRC).

There are only 880 mountain gorillas left in the wild and their habitat is under threat because of illegal mining for coltan. Coltan is a valuable mineral. It is used in mobile phones. Eighty per cent of the world's coltan is in DRC. There's even illegal mining taking place in a UNESCO World Heritage park (the Kahuzi-Biega National Park). This park is the last place in the wild to find eastern lowland gorillas.

Miners are taking over farmland too. Farmers then have no way to earn money so they poach gorillas and sell the meat (bushmeat) to miners and rebel armies. This is a further threat to the survival of gorilla species in the wild.

Don't throw your old mobile in the garbage!

We can refurbish and resell your old mobile phone or recycle its valuable parts.

Donate it to the school and we will happily use it for a good cause—Gorilla Doctors.

1. Old mobile phones are
   - **A** donated to the Gorilla Doctors.
   - **B** refurbished, resold or recycled.
   - **C** thrown in the garbage.
   - **D** repaired and returned to owners.
2. Who are the Gorilla Doctors?
   - **A** vets who wear gorilla costumes
   - **B** vets who care for gorillas
   - **C** doctors who are gorillas
   - **D** doctors who work in places such as DRC
3. To 'poach' gorillas means
   - **A** to sell them.
   - **B** to capture them.
   - **C** to cook them.
   - **D** to kill them.
4. Choose all that apply. The illegal mining
   - **A** is against the law.
   - **B** shouldn't be happening.
   - **C** displaces farmers.
   - **D** means that gorillas are in trouble.
5. Choose all that apply. Why does illegal mining take place?
   - **A** Coltan is valuable.
   - **B** Mobile phones need coltan.
   - **C** Farms are being destroyed.
   - **D** People want mobile phones.
6. Why is recycling coltan important?

   ....

   ....

   ....

Spelling

Rewrite the misspelt words.

1 Mining in the national park is ilegal.

2 Farmers are also loosing their land to mining.

3 Recycle old mobial phones.

4 Gorilla habatat is being lost to mining.

5 Write three words from the word family that includes **threat**.

Vocabulary

Circle the word that has the nearest meaning to the underlined word.

6 Coltan is a valuable mineral.

A expensive B cheap
C economical D discounted

7 Coltan mining is a threat to the survival of gorillas.

A happiness B existence
C death D extinction

8 Add a word from the text to the sentence.

Don't put recyclable things in the ______.

9 Write a word from the text to match the meaning.

the process of getting minerals from the ground ______

Circle the word on each line that does **not** belong.

10 precious treasured valuable cheap

11 support help hinder aid

Grammar

12 Complete the sentence with a four-word noun group from the text.

Our school can recycle ______ ______ ______ ______.

13 Complete the sentence with a relating (being or having) verb from the text.

Gorilla habitat ______ under threat.

14 Choose the correct adverb to complete the sentence.

We will (sadly / happily / noisily) make sure your old phone goes to a good cause.

15 Use a connective from the box to complete the sentence correctly.

As well as	Then	Therefore	Unless

______ we save their habitat there will be no gorillas left in the wild.

Punctuation

16 Circle the sentence that is punctuated correctly.

A Most of the worlds Coltan is in africa.
B Most of the worlds coltan is in Africa
C Most of the world's coltan is in Africa.

Rewrite each sentence correctly.

17 farmers with no income sell gorilla meat

18 the organisation is called gorilla doctors

UNIT 17A

Reading and Comprehension

Escape

Arthur ate his lunch as quickly as he could so that he could spend the rest of lunchtime in the library.

It was cool in the library and the light was dim. He settled on the floor, his back against the shelf of books. He felt very comfortable. He started reading and soon forgot where he was.

The story he had started earlier in the week was set in the countryside many years ago. He was up to the part in the story where Sophia and Angus had just been told that their uncle would arrive soon to take them to live with him in the city. Their mother was ill and they could not stay on their farm. The children had protested loudly. They did not want to go to live with their uncle. They did not want to leave their farm.

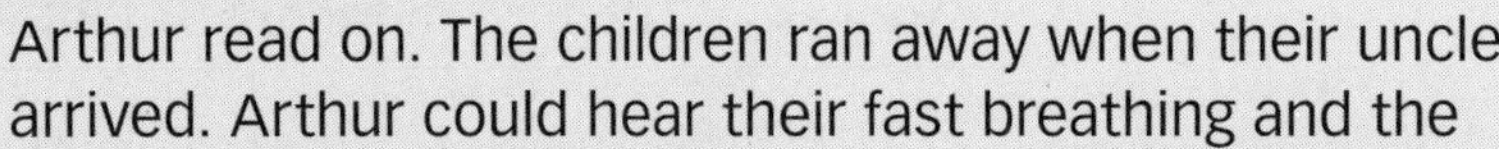

Arthur read on. The children ran away when their uncle arrived. Arthur could hear their fast breathing and the thump of their feet on the ground. He could feel the wind dragging at their clothes. He heard them yell for Banjo to follow them. He felt their hearts pounding in their chests.

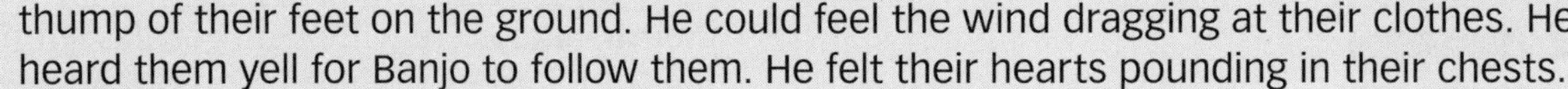

'Quickly,' he said. 'Hide.'

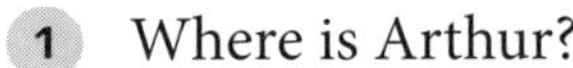

1. Where is Arthur?
   - A on a shelf
   - B on a farm
   - C at lunchtime
   - D in the school library

2. Arthur was reading a story about
   - A an uncle in the city.
   - B two children.
   - C a farm.
   - D a sick mother.

3. ‘‘Quickly,’ he said. ‘Hide.’‘ Who said this?
   - A Arthur
   - B Sophia
   - C the mother
   - D Angus

4. Banjo in the story is the children's
   - A dog.
   - B dad.
   - C mum.
   - D uncle.

5. How does Arthur feel about the story?
   - A too worried about the children to read any more
   - B excited and interested
   - C interested but tired of reading
   - D fascinated about farm life

6. What sort of story is Arthur reading?
   - A a funny story
   - B a spooky story
   - C an adventure story
   - D a sad story

Spelling

Rewrite the misspelt words.

1 The lite was dim.

2 He felt very comftable.

3 They didn't want to live with their unkel.

4 The wind was dragging at their cloths.

5 Write three words from the word family that includes **quick**.

Vocabulary

Circle the word that has the nearest meaning to the underlined word.

6 The children had protested.

A argued B grumbled
C agreed D celebrated

7 Arthur had started reading the book earlier in the week.

A finished B continued
C commenced D disliked

8 Add a word from the text to the sentence.

The temperature was ______ in the library.

9 Write a word from the text to match the meaning.

a place where books, CDs, films and other items are kept for borrowing ______

Circle the word on each line that does **not** belong.

10 dragging pulling pushing tugging

11 call yell shout murmur

Grammar

12 Complete the sentence with an article.

Arthur sat on ______ floor.

13 Complete the sentence with a relating (being or having) verb from the text.

Their mother ______ ill.

14 Complete the sentence with an adverb from the text to tell **how**.

The children had protested ______.

15 Use a connective from the box to complete the sentence correctly.

When	Then	While	Next	Eventually

______ their uncle arrived, the children ran away.

Punctuation

16 Circle the sentence that is punctuated correctly.

A Is it a good book? asked the library teacher.

B 'Is it a good book?' asked the library teacher.

C 'Is it a good book? asked the library teacher.'

Rewrite each sentence correctly.

17 quickly he said

18 arthur read a library book

Reading and Comprehension

A happy ending for a Boobook

My nana is a wildlife volunteer. She volunteers because she loves animals. She looks after native birds that are injured. She cares for them at her home.

A few months ago she had to look after a young Southern Boobook owl. It was found on the ground under a tree. It couldn't fly and its parents were nowhere to be seen. The rescuer was worried that a dog or cat might hurt it so he phoned my nana's group. Someone met him, collected the bird and quickly brought it to my nana.

Boobooks are Australia's smallest owl. They are sometimes called 'mopokes'. Nana had to teach the Boobook what to eat. Once it could fly Nana took it to the wild bird rehabilitation centre where there is a large aviary in which the birds live until they are fully healthy. The Boobook was able to practise flying and catching moths to eat.

One night, after three weeks in the aviary, it was ready to fend for itself in the bush. Nana and the other carers released it next to the same tree where it was found.

Nana was very happy to see her 'baby' fly free. She used an infrared camera to watch it land on the branch of a tall tree.

1. Nana is
   - **A** a Southern Boobook.
   - **B** a wildlife volunteer.
   - **C** a bird feeder.
   - **D** a wildlife specialist.

2. How long did the Boobook spend in the aviary?
   - **A** a few months
   - **B** until it grew up
   - **C** three weeks
   - **D** while it was only young

3. What happens during rehabilitation?
   - **A** Birds become stronger and healthier.
   - **B** Birds learn to catch moths.
   - **C** Vets mend their injuries.
   - **D** Birds eat a lot.

4. Why did Nana use an infrared camera?
   - **A** to see at night
   - **B** to take photos
   - **C** to see all the trees
   - **D** to look out for injured birds

5. The Boobook was released where it was found
   - **A** because the man who found it wanted to see it released.
   - **B** so Nana could watch.
   - **C** because the carers knew that spot.
   - **D** because that was its natural territory.

6. How does Nana feel about being a volunteer?

   ....

   ....

   ....

Spelling

Rewrite the misspelt words.

1 She volenteers to help animals.

2 The parents were nowear to be seen.

3 The bird was releesed into the bush.

4 Nana helps at the rehabilitashun centre.

5 Write three words from the word family that includes **injured**.

Vocabulary

Circle the word that has the nearest meaning to the underlined word.

6 Sometimes birds are injured by cats and dogs.
- A upset
- B killed
- C hurt
- D wrecked

7 Carers took it to the tree where it was found.
- A discovered
- B lost
- C revealed
- D taken

8 Add a word from the text to the sentence.
Birds recover at the ______ centre.

9 Write a word from the text to match the meaning.
an enclosure for birds ______

Circle the word on each line that does **not** belong.

10 phoned contacted wrote agreed

11 wild free caged natural

Grammar

12 Complete the sentence with a five-word noun group from the text.
Nana took the owl to ______ ______ ______ ______ ______.

13 Complete the sentence with a relating (being or having) verb from the text.
Nana ______ a volunteer.

14 Complete the sentence with an adverb from the text to tell **how**.
Someone ______ brought the injured bird to Nana.

15 Use a connective from the box to complete the sentence correctly.

as well as	then	therefore	unless

There's no point releasing a bird ______ it can fend for itself in the wild.

Punctuation

16 Circle the sentence that is punctuated correctly.
- A Nana cared for a southern boobook owl
- B Nana cared for a Southern Boobook owl.
- C Nana cared for a southern Boobook owl.

Rewrite each sentence correctly.

17 nanas group cares for injured birds

18 the little owl couldnt fly

Fairtrade

You can find the word 'Fairtrade' and a Fairtrade symbol on items such as chocolate, coffee and tea when you go shopping. When you find something in a shop that says it's Fairtrade you know that the producers of the goods—farmers in developing countries—have been treated fairly and that they are paid a fair price for their goods. Fairtrade helps workers get safe working conditions. Fairtrade protects the environment too.

In Samoa, Fairtrade Australia and New Zealand (ANZ) has been working with coconut farmers. The farmers have been taught how to improve their soil. Better soil means that they can grow more coconuts and improve the quality of their coconuts. Farmers have also been given farming tools such as wheelbarrows and pruning shears.

In a remote area of Papua New Guinea, Fairtrade ANZ has worked with cocoa growers. Cocoa is used to make chocolate. Fairtrade ANZ has helped to improve the everyday lives of the farmers, getting them a fair price for their cocoa, access to doctors and schooling for the children.

1 In the text Fairtrade helped coconut farmers in
- A Australia.
- B New Zealand.
- C Papua New Guinea.
- D Samoa.

2 The farmers in Papua New Guinea grow
- A coconuts.
- B cocoa.
- C chocolate.
- D coffee and tea.

3 Choose all that apply. Wheelbarrows and pruning shears
- A make farm work easier.
- B aren't helpful on a coconut farm.
- C probably cost too much for farmers in developing countries.
- D might not be available in remote areas of Samoa.

4 How would farmers feel about Fairtrade?
- A glad for the support and advice
- B pleased with the help but would prefer to grow coffee
- C not happy about being told what to do
- D tired of all the work

5 How can Fairtrade improve lives? Choose all that apply.
- A helping with access to doctors and schools
- B supporting fair wages
- C buying better quality soil
- D making tastier chocolate

6 What do you think of Fairtrade?

....

....

....

Spelling

Rewrite the misspelt words.

1. Cocoa is used to make <u>choclate</u>.

   ....

2. Fairtrade helps farmers in developing <u>countreys</u>.

   ....

3. The farmers are <u>tort</u> helpful skills.

   ....

4. Fairtrade helps the <u>enviroment</u>.

   ....

5. Write three words from the word family that includes **protect**.

   ....

   ....

   ....

Vocabulary

Circle the word that has the nearest meaning to the underlined word.

6. Farmers are <u>producers</u> of goods.
   - A workers
   - B growers
   - C manufacturers
   - D helpers

7. Some cocoa farmers live in <u>remote</u> areas.
   - A local
   - B isolated
   - C nearby
   - D farming

8. Add a word from the text to the sentence.

   Look for a Fairtrade .... on items when shopping.

9. Write a word from the text to match the meaning.

   equipment that helps with work

   ....

Circle the word on each line that does **not** belong.

10. ruin improve destroy worsen

11. soil dust earth dirt

Grammar

12. Complete the sentence with an article.

    Fairtrade helps farmers get .... fair price for the produce.

13. Choose the correct relating (being or having) verb to complete the sentence.

    Farmers (is / was / are) hard workers.

14. Complete the sentence with an adverb from the text to tell **how**.

    Farmers should be treated ....

15. Use a connective from the box to complete the sentence correctly.

As well as	Then	Therefore	Unless

....

access to doctors, Fairtrade can help with access to schooling.

Punctuation

16. Circle the sentence that is punctuated correctly.
    - A It's good to support Fairtrade farmers.
    - B Its good to support Fairtrade farmers.
    - C Its good to support fairtrade farmers.

Rewrite each sentence correctly.

17. farmers in papua new guinea grow cocoa

    ....

    ....

    ....

18. fairtrade anz works in samoa

    ....

    ....

    ....

Reading and Comprehension

Odelia returns

Odelia walked quickly along the dirt track to school. She was excited. She had been absent for over a month. She hoped she had not missed too much work but she was confident the teacher would help her catch up. Children in her class were often absent from school for long periods of time. The teacher was always happy to see them return.

Odelia's mother was a cocoa farmer in Papua New Guinea. Their small farm had seen troubles recently because a pest had attacked the cocoa bean pods. Odelia's mother had been worried that they might have to give up farming cocoa altogether. Odelia had helped her mother plant taro, just in case.

The Fairtrade people had told Odelia's mother and the other cocoa farmers in the district to erect shades for the cocoa trees and to bury the diseased pods. They said that borer larvae feed inside the bean pod so burying the pods would break the borer's life cycle. Once Odelia's mother learned how to kill the borers she knew her farm was saved. Odelia was able to return to school at last.

Odelia reached the schoolyard. She saw her friend Marta and ran towards her.

1. How does Odelia get to school?
   - **A** in a wheelbarrow
   - **B** on a pushbike
   - **C** on a horse
   - **D** by walking

2. What grows on Odelia's farm?
   - **A** coconuts and cocoa
   - **B** cocoa borers, cocoa and taro
   - **C** cocoa and taro
   - **D** cocoa

3. Note the title of the text. Where does Odelia return?
   - **A** to the cocoa trees
   - **B** to the farm
   - **C** to school
   - **D** to her mother

4. They planted taro 'just in case' of what?
   - **A** The borer larvae were inside the cocoa pods.
   - **B** Odelia was hungry.
   - **C** The borers ate all the taro.
   - **D** All the cocoa pods were destroyed.

5. Why had Odelia missed school?
   - **A** She didn't like school.
   - **B** She'd been helping on the farm.
   - **C** Her mother did not make her go to school.
   - **D** She had a holiday.

6. Would you like to live Odelia's life? Why or why not?

   ....

   ....

   ....

Spelling

Rewrite the misspelt words.

1 Odelia walked kwickly.

2 Their farm had seen trubbles recently.

3 Odelia's mother had been wurried.

4 The cocoa pods were deseased.

5 Write three words from the word family that includes **excited**.

Vocabulary

Circle the word that has the nearest meaning to the underlined word.

6 Odelia was confident the teacher would help her.

A happy B ready
C sure D brave

7 Borer larvae feed inside the bean pod.

A spoil B eat
C are eaten D ruin

8 Add a word from the text to the sentence.

Children in the district were often ______ from school.

9 Write a word from the text to match the meaning.

something that harms crops ______

Circle the word on each line that does **not** belong.

10 excited happy worried thrilled

11 attacking destroying killing helping

Grammar

12 Complete the sentence with a three-word noun group from the text.

______ ______ ______ had told Odelia's mother how to save her farm.

13 Choose the correct relating (being or having) verb to complete the sentence.

Odelia (is / was / are) excited.

14 Complete the sentence with an adverb from the text to tell **how**.

Odelia walked ______ to school.

15 Use a connective from the box to complete the sentence correctly.

as well as	then	therefore	unless

Odelia's mother erected shades and

______

she buried the seed pods.

Punctuation

16 Circle the sentence that is punctuated correctly.

A Odelia's friend had missed her.
B Odelias friend had missed her.
C Odelia's friend had missed her

Rewrite each sentence correctly.

17 odelias mother is a farmer

18 odelia lives in papua new guinea

Reading and Comprehension

Tree-mendous project

Children around the globe are planting trees as part of the 'One Tree Per Child' project, launched in 2015 by Olivia Newton-John and Jon Dee.

The idea of the 'One Tree Per Child' project is for every primary schoolchild across the world to plant a tree as part of a school activity. The project started as a seed of an idea and now has branches around the world. Villages, towns and cities in Australia, Africa, England, Europe and USA have joined the project. Millions of trees have been planted. Some communities have proudly exceeded the 'One Tree Per Child' target.

Numerous local government councils in Australia are assisting with funding or providing suitable tree species to schools and community groups to plant in appropriate local areas.

The benefits of the project are numerous. Trees make oxygen for all animals to breathe. They store carbon and therefore help to prevent climate change. They provide homes for wildlife.

The project gets children involved in volunteering in their own communities and proves that small acts can make a huge difference to the world.
For more information visit www.onetreeperchild.com.

1 Why would you visit the website?
- A to speak with Olivia Newton-John
- B to learn which trees to plant
- C for more information about the project
- D to get free trees

2 How do trees prevent climate change?
- A They store carbon.
- B They make carbon.
- C They grow carbon.
- D They release carbon.

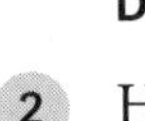

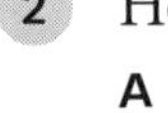
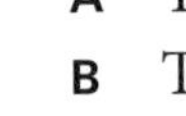

3 Local councils in Australia are
- A competing with countries around the world.
- B planting trees in each area.
- C doing what the government tells them to do.
- D supporting the project.

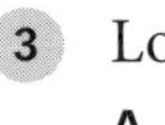
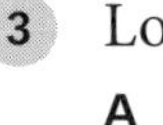
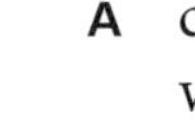
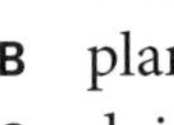
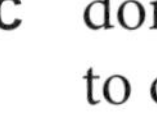
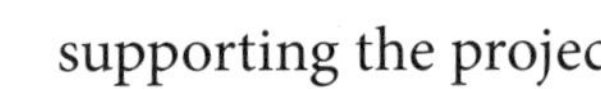

4 It's a school activity
- A so teachers do the work.
- B because teachers like planting trees.
- C so more trees get planted.
- D so that children play outdoors.

5 Which do you think is most important?
- A Trees provide homes for wildlife.
- B Trees prevent climate change.
- C Trees make oxygen.
- D Children become volunteers.

6 Would you like your school to be part of this project? Explain your answer.

....

....

....

....

Spelling

Rewrite the misspelt words.

1 Children around the <u>werld</u> are planting trees.

2 Plant a tree as part of a school <u>activitiy</u>.

3 Some <u>communiteys</u> have planted lots of trees.

4 The benefits of the project are <u>numerus</u>.

5 Write three words from the word family that includes **government**.

Vocabulary

Circle the word that has the nearest meaning to the underlined word.

6 <u>Numerous</u> councils are assisting with funding.

A Some B Many
C All D Lots

7 <u>Suitable</u> trees are provided for local areas.

A Sustainable B Rare
C Appropriate D Proper

8 Add a word from the text to the sentence.

The ______________________ of the project are numerous.

9 Write a word from the text to match the meaning.

advantages ______________________

Circle the word on each line that does **not** belong.

10 assisting supporting helping preventing

11 giving taking offering volunteering

Grammar

12 Complete the sentence with a two-word noun group from the text.

__________ __________ started as a seed of an idea.

13 Choose the correct relating (being or having) verb to complete the sentence.

The benefits (was / were / are) numerous.

14 Complete the sentence with an adverb from the text to tell **how**.

Some communities have ______________ exceeded their target.

15 Use a connective from the box to complete the sentence correctly.

as well as	then	therefore	unless

Trees store carbon and

____

help prevent climate change.

Punctuation

16 Circle the sentence that is punctuated correctly.

A 'Its important to plant trees' said Olivia.
B It's important to plant trees, said Olivia.
C 'It's important to plant trees,' said Olivia.

Rewrite each sentence correctly.

17 the project was launched by olivia newton-john and jon dee

18 its a tremendous project said the teacher

Reading and Comprehension

Silkworm farming

Silk is made by silkworms. Silkworm farming is called sericulture.

When the silkworm hatches from an egg it is thin and black. Over the next month the worm eats a large amount of mulberry leaves and grows very fat. Then it spins a silk cocoon around itself. This takes about 48 hours. The cocoon is a single strand of silk and it can be 900 m in length. Inside the cocoon the worm moults and changes into a pupa.

After about 10 days the pupa inside the cocoon has turned into a moth. The moth releases enzymes to dissolve a hole in the silk so it can crawl out. The silkworm moth cannot eat and does not fly. It flutters around searching for a mate. The moth only lives briefly, just long enough to breed. The male dies soon after mating. The female dies after laying her eggs.

In most silkworm farming the cocoon is boiled to kill the pupa. If the pupa is allowed to transform into a moth the silk thread will be damaged by the moth's enzymes.

Some people object to the practice of boiling the pupa. These people refuse to buy silk farmed like this. They buy 'peace silk' where the moth is allowed to emerge for breeding and then dies naturally.

1 How is silk made?
- A Spiders spin it.
- B It's made in cocoons.
- C The silkworm spins it.
- D People spin it.

2 A silkworm is a pupa for
- A two days.
- B a month.
- C 21 days.
- D 10 days.

3 In most silkworm farming why isn't the moth allowed out of its cocoon?
- A It will breed.
- B Damaged silk is less valuable.
- C The eggs will be lost.
- D It can't fly and will get hurt.

4 The silkworm spends most of its life
- A as a moth.
- B eating.
- C in a cocoon.
- D spinning.

5 What do you think of the life cycle of the silkworm?
- A short but sweet
- B sad and lonely
- C short and lazy
- D busy but lonely

6 Why would people object to silkworm farming practices?

....

....

....

Spelling

Rewrite the misspelt words.

1 Silkworms molt.

....

2 Silkworms spin cucoons.

....

3 The moth's enzymes dezolve the silk.

....

4 Moths make a whole in the cocoon.

....

5 Write three words from the word family that includes **allowed**.

....

....

....

Vocabulary

Circle the word that has the nearest meaning to the underlined word.

6 The moth's enzymes dissolve a hole in the silk.

A chew **B** melt
C create **D** dig

7 The worm spins a cocoon.

A bubble **B** coat
C case **D** nest

8 Add a word from the text to the sentence.

A pupa will .... into a moth.

9 Write a word from the text to match the meaning.

something made by an animal to perform a specific function ....

Circle the word on each line that does **not** belong.

10 hatches disappears emerges appears

11 dies lives exists survives

Grammar

12 Complete the sentence with a four-word noun group from the text.

....
.... will be damaged by the moth's enzymes.

13 Choose the correct relating (being or having) verb to complete the sentence.

Em (were / are / was) sad to see so many animals waiting for forever homes.

14 Complete the sentence with an adverb from the text to tell **how**.

In the production of 'peace silk' the moth dies ....

15 Use a connective from the box to complete the sentence correctly.

as well as	then	therefore	unless

The male mates and .... dies.

Punctuation

16 Circle the sentence that is punctuated correctly.

A 'Pick some mulberry leaves,' said Mum.
B Pick some mulberry leaves, 'said Mum.'
C 'Pick some mulberry leaves,' said Mum

Rewrite each sentence correctly.

17 the silkworms cocoon is made of silk

....

....

....

18 my silkworms have hatched said oliver

....

....

....

Reading and Comprehension

Our forever home

To: nanandpa.shipway@gmail.com

Hello Nan and Pa

We finally got a dog. We adopted one from the RSPCA. We went online to their website. Their website features all the animals that are waiting for forever homes. It was sad to see so many.

The good thing about adopting a pet from a shelter is that all the animals have been desexed, microchipped, vaccinated, and are treated for worms and fleas.

The other useful thing is that shelter staff can answer questions about whether a particular animal would be suited to your home, your lifestyle, your family, your budget, and so on. They say it's important to choose a pet that suits you. Mum says that people choosing the wrong pet for their situation is one of the reasons that animal shelters end up with so many pets needing to be rehomed.

Mum, Paul and I looked carefully online first. Then Paul and I went to the shelter to meet the dogs. Mum had to go to work but said she trusted us with the decision. We chose Panda.

We'll all visit you soon, love Em

1. Which website did Em, Paul and Mum use?
   - **A** all animal shelter websites
   - **B** the RSPCA's
   - **C** homeless animal websites
   - **D** the RSACP's

2. It was 'sad to see so many'
   - **A** homeless animals.
   - **B** homeless dogs.
   - **C** lost pets.
   - **D** dogs that need forever homes.

3. What decision did Mum trust Paul and Em with?
   - **A** to get a pet
   - **B** which dog to choose
   - **C** to go to the shelter without her
   - **D** where to get a dog

4. Why do you think the animal was named Panda?
   - **A** It was a panda bear.
   - **B** It had black and white fur.
   - **C** It was fat and fluffy.
   - **D** It ate bamboo.

5. Choose all that apply. An example of a wrong pet for a situation would be
   - **A** an energetic dog with an unenergetic owner.
   - **B** a big dog on a farm.
   - **C** an energetic dog with an energetic owner.
   - **D** a cat with an owner who is allergic to cat fur.

6. How do you find the right match?

   ....

   ....

Spelling

Rewrite the misspelt words.

1 We desided to adopt a pet.

2 It's yuseful that staff can answer questions.

3 A particula animal might suit you better.

4 Chewzing the right pet is important.

5 Write three words from the word family that includes **suit**.

Vocabulary

Circle the word that has the nearest meaning to the underlined word.

6 It was sad to see so many homeless pets.
   A upsetting B heartless
   C cruel D pointless

7 The website features all the animals.
   A offers B displays
   C films D describes

8 Add a word from the text to the sentence.
   All RSPCA animals have been ______ for fleas and worms.

9 Write a word from the text to match the meaning.
   a place where pets wait to be rehomed

Circle the word on each line that does **not** belong.

10 wrong correct inappropriate unsuitable

11 decision problem choice verdict

Grammar

12 Complete the sentence with a four-word noun group from the text.
   ______ ______ ______ ______ looked online first.

13 Choose the correct relating (being or having) verb to complete the sentence.
   All the animals ______ treated for worms and fleas.

14 Complete the sentence with an adverb from the text to tell **how**.
   Mum, Paul and I looked ______ online first.

15 Use a connective from the box to complete the sentence correctly.

as well as	then	therefore	unless

   Think about the particular animal ______ your situation, before choosing a pet.

Punctuation

16 Circle the sentence that is punctuated correctly.
   A 'Paul said, Let's get a dog.'
   B Paul said 'Let's get a dog'
   C Paul said, 'Let's get a dog.'

Rewrite each sentence correctly.

17 we decided wed adopt a pet

18 mum said I trust you to choose

Reading and Comprehension

Write a noun from the box in each space.

chocolate	Doctors	school	owl	moths
phones	money	tea	coffee	gorillas

1 Donate mobile ____________ to save ____________. Our ____________ will recycle them and donate the ____________ to Gorilla ____________.

2 Boobooks are a kind of ____________. They eat ____________.

3 Fairtrade goods include ____________, ____________ and ____________.

Write a verb from the box in each space.

hatch	give	make	eat	choose	transform	spin	grow	adopt	store

4 Silkworms ____________ from eggs. They ____________ mulberry leaves and ____________ fat, then they ____________ cocoons. They ____________ into moths.

5 You can ____________ a pet from an animal shelter. You need to ____________ wisely.

6 Trees ____________ oxygen and ____________ carbon.

7 Volunteers ____________ their time.

Spelling

The spelling mistakes in these sentences have been circled. Write the correct spelling on the lines.

8 Recycle old (mobial) phones. ____________

9 Gorilla (habatat) is being lost to mining. ____________

10 Mining in the national park is (ilegal). ____________

11 Fairtrade helps farmers in developing (countreys). ____________

12 Fairtrade helps the (enviroment). ____________

13 Some (communiteys) have planted lots of trees. ____________

14 It's cool and (comftable) in the library. ____________

15 Silkworms have a four-stage life (cycel). ____________

Vocabulary

16 Circle the correct word in the brackets.
There was a (whole / hole) in the cocoon.

17 Circle the word that is the opposite of **like**.
love admire dislike

Grammar

18 Add a noun to the sentence.
Silkworm moths emerge from ________________________.

19 Add a relating (being or having) verb to the sentence.
Trees ________________________ homes for wildlife.

20 Add an adverb to tell **how**.
The children were told to finish their work ________________________.

21 Add a pronoun to the sentence.
Cooper and Sally hurried home because ________________________ wanted to walk their dog.

22 Add a connective to the sentence.
The teacher said, 'You've finished your work ______________________________ you have time to read.'

Punctuation

Rewrite each sentence correctly.

23 its time for reading said the teacher

____

____

24 is that a good book asked the teacher

____

____

25 cocoa is grown in papua new guinea

____

____

NAPLAN-STYLE

3

READING TEST

Reading

The search for Rangor

This is an extract from a narrative. Rangor is the name of a place.

It had four strong legs and two huge wings. The wings had sharp points. It had a long, scaly tail ending in a point. Its feet had three sharp claws. Its head had horns. It had sharp teeth and angry eyes. It was a fearsome dragon.

Rama stood her ground. She knew that if she turned her back on the animal it would pounce on her and kill her with its sharp claws and teeth. She'd seen that happen to a friend. She stood tall and stared it in the eyes.

It was frozen in place, breathing steam through its flared nostrils. It was summing her up but seemed confused. It must have been thinking, 'What is this puny thing in front of me? Why doesn't it run away? It must be very powerful to stand there unafraid.'

It snorted. The wind from its nostrils almost blew her over but she stood her ground in silence. Then eventually it turned and walked away from Rama, back into the entrance of the cave.

Now Rama could breathe.

1. The dragon's tail ended in
   - **A** scales.
   - **B** wings.
   - **C** sharp claws.
   - **D** a point.

2. Eventually the dragon walked
   - **A** into a cave.
   - **B** up a mountain.
   - **C** over to Rama.
   - **D** across the ground.

3. How did Rama know to stand her ground?
   - **A** past experience
   - **B** Someone had taught her.
   - **C** instinct
   - **D** The dragon told her.

4. Choose all that apply. Why was the dragon confused?
   - **A** Steam was coming from its nostrils.
   - **B** Rama did not turn and run away.
   - **C** The puny thing did not show fear.
   - **D** Rama looked very powerful.

5. Why could Rama breathe at the end?
   - **A** because the dragon snorted
   - **B** because the dragon was summing her up
   - **C** because the danger was over
   - **D** because the dragon almost blew her over

6. This text is part of
   - **A** a historical narrative.
   - **B** a biography.
   - **C** a science-fiction story.
   - **D** a fantasy adventure story.

7. Would you like to read more about Rama? Why or why not?

NAPLAN-STYLE 3 CONVENTIONS OF LANGUAGE TEST

Spelling

The spelling mistakes in these sentences have been underlined.
Write the correct spelling on the lines.

1 Its feet had three sharp clawes. ______________________

2 It was a fearsum dragon. ______________________

3 It was breething steam through its nostrils. ______________________

4 The dragon was very powafull. ______________________

Vocabulary

5 Which word means **to be unsure or puzzled**?

A dazed B dizzy C confident D confused

6 Which word does **not** belong?

A strong B puny C mighty D powerful

7 Which word does **not** belong?

A fearsome B scary C ordinary D impressive

Grammar

8 Which adjective describes the dragon?

A weak B terrifying C pleasant D unimportant

9 Which verb or verb group completes the sentence correctly.

It ______________ a fearsome dragon.

A is being B were C was D had been

10 Which adverb completes the sentence to tell **how**?

Rama stared ______________ at the dragon.

A brave B bravely C bravest D braver

Punctuation

11 Which sentence is punctuated correctly?

A 'What is this puny thing?' thought the dragon.

B Why doesn't it run away? 'thought the dragon'.

C It must be powerful thought, the dragon.

12 Which sentence is punctuated correctly?

A 'I will stand my ground.' thought Rama.

B 'I will not show fear,' thought Rama.

C 'I will stare it in the eyes thought,' Rama.

Reading and Comprehension

Nowhere else to be

Jack arrived at school. He was cold. He had grown out of his school jumper and there'd been nothing at home for breakfast.

He moved around the side of the building to get out of the wind. It was also better to hide from any teachers even though he doubted any would be at school yet. Playground supervision commenced at 8:30. Children weren't meant to arrive two hours early.

His stomach rumbled. He thought about what he'd buy to eat if he had some money. If he had a dollar he could get a banana at the corner store. Maybe he should look around the playground for lost coins. Instead, he had a long drink from the bubbler outside the locked toilet block.

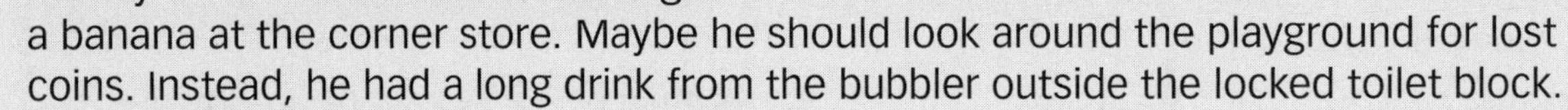

Eric would arrive just after 8:30. Eric usually had something for him to eat. Eric's mum often commented that Eric had hollow legs. Jack was lucky he had a friend like Eric. Eric might also have a spare jumper.

1. Who was Eric?
   - **A** Jack's friend
   - **B** Jack's neighbour
   - **C** Jack's brother
   - **D** a teacher

2. What did Jack want for breakfast?
   - **A** nothing
   - **B** water
   - **C** a banana
   - **D** cereal

3. What time did Jack arrive at school?
   - **A** 8:30
   - **B** 6:30
   - **C** 10:30
   - **D** 7:30

4. Jack had a drink instead of what?
   - **A** going to the toilet
   - **B** looking for lost coins
   - **C** buying a banana
   - **D** eating breakfast

5. Why didn't Jack have a jumper?
   - **A** His family could not afford to buy one.
   - **B** He'd lost it.
   - **C** Eric had it.
   - **D** Someone had stolen it.

6. Choose the best description of Eric.
   - **A** loyal and proud
   - **B** hungry and thoughtful
   - **C** dependable and good at schoolwork
   - **D** thoughtful and dependable

Spelling

Rewrite the misspelt words.

1 The boy arived at school.

2 He moved to the side of the bilding.

3 Children wernt meant to be at school so early.

4 His stomick rumbled.

5 Write three words from the word family that includes **supervision**.

Vocabulary

Circle the word that has the nearest meaning to the underlined word.

6 Playground supervision commenced at 8:30.

A finished B began
C ended D arrived

7 Eric must have hollow legs.

A useless B empty
C thin D fat

8 Add a word from the text to the sentence.

You need .... to buy things.

9 Write a word from the text to match the meaning.

to be fortunate ....

Circle the word on each line that does **not** belong.

10 commenced ended started began

11 lost misplaced stolen forgotten

Grammar

12 Complete the sentence with a noun group from the text.

.... rumbled.

13 Complete the sentence with a saying verb from the text.

Eric's mum often .... that Eric had hollow legs.

14 Complete the sentence with an adverbial phrase from the text.

He drank from the bubbler

....

15 Use a connective from the box to complete the sentence correctly.

also	next	consequently	alternatively

Jack had no jumper and

....

he was cold.

Punctuation

16 Circle the sentence that is punctuated correctly.

A 'Did you bring something to eat,' asked Jack.

B 'Did you bring something,' to eat asked jack.

C 'Did you bring something to eat?' asked Jack.

Rewrite each sentence correctly.

17 he'd wait for eric

18 hello eric said jack

Reading and Comprehension

Warragamba News

News Sport Business Politics Lifestyle Travel Cars

A SPLASHY opening!

The new Upton Street Aquatic Centre had its grand opening on Saturday.

The state-of-the-art centre features a 50-m x 10-lane main pool, suitable for national swimming titles and other events. There is also a gym, toddler's play pool and a children's 25-m lap pool (ideal for lessons).

Happy nine-year-old local Sofie Ray has signed up for the under 10 swim squad. She praised the centre, saying, 'It's amazing. I used to have lessons at Kingsway but it's so far away. This pool is awesome!'

There is also a 10-m rehabilitation pool. 'The rehabilitation pool is a bonus for people with disabilities or people recovering from an injury or a medical problem,' said on-site physiotherapist Felicity Anwar.

Soul Café serves healthy foods and beverages, including smoothies and vegetable juices, to keep you feeling energetic.

Construction of the aquatic centre began two years ago. Its design is the result of extensive community consultation. The centre is open seven days a week from 5 am until 9 pm all year round.

1 How long did the centre take to build?
- A nine years
- B 10 months
- C two years
- D Saturday

2 The rehabilitation pool is for
- A toddlers.
- B children's lessons.
- C people with disabilities.
- D national swimming titles.

3 The new centre was designed for
- A children's parties.
- B swimming.
- C eating.
- D entertaining.

4 The physiotherapist
- A teaches toddlers to swim.
- B gives swimming lessons.
- C works in Soul Café.
- D works with people who have injuries.

5 'Extensive community consultation' means that
- A the pool was designed by experts.
- B the community location was considered.
- C lots of people were asked for ideas.
- D the centre is an awesome design.

6 Is there anyone who would not use the centre? Explain your answer.

____

____

____

Spelling

Rewrite the misspelt words.

1 Natonial swimming titles can be held.

....

2 The centre is suitible for lessons.

....

3 Buy vegtable juice at the café.

....

4 Refuel to feel enerjetic.

....

5 Write three words from the word family that includes **disabilities**.

....

....

....

Vocabulary

Circle the word that has the nearest meaning to the underlined word.

6 It was designed after extensive consultation.

A obvious B deliberate
C wide D useful

7 The cafe serves food and beverages.

A tickets B drinks
C souvenirs D bonuses

8 Add a word from the text to the sentence.

The centre is .... seven days a week.

9 Write a word from the text to match the meaning.

the action of building something

....

Circle the word on each line that does **not** belong.

10 amazing awful awesome wonderful

11 bonus advantage benefit disadvantage

Grammar

12 Complete the sentence with a noun group from the text.

.... will give you energy.

13 Complete the sentence with a saying verb from the text.

Sofie .... the Centre.

14 Complete the sentence with an adverbial phrase.

The grand opening was ....

15 Use a connective from the box to complete the sentence correctly.

also	next	consequently	alternatively

The centre is amazing, ... children want to have swimming lessons there.

Punctuation

16 Circle the sentence that is punctuated correctly.

A 'I love it here!' commented Sofie.
B I love it here 'commented Sofie!'
C 'I love it here,' commented Sofie!

Rewrite each sentence correctly.

17 the pool is amazing said felicity

....

....

....

18 sofie ray has joined the swim squad

....

....

....

Reading and Comprehension

My hero

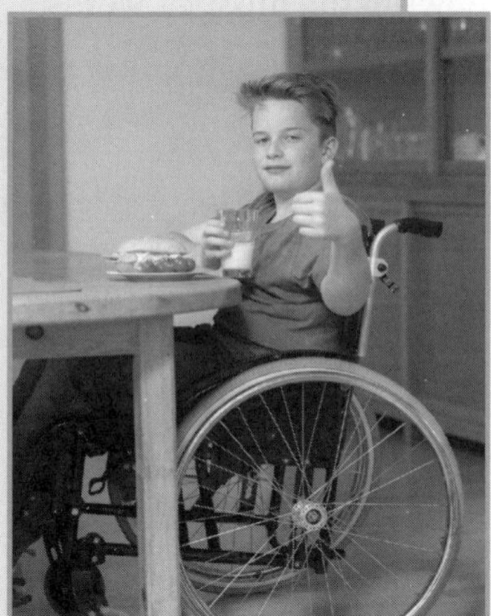

When I grow up I want to be a tennis champion. I want to win as many medals for tennis as Louise Sauvage has won for racing.

Louise Sauvage is my sporting hero. She has been competing internationally in track and field events since 1990. She has won countless medals including a gold medal at the Olympic Games in Sydney and two gold medals and a silver at the Paralympics. She has won the Boston marathon multiple times.

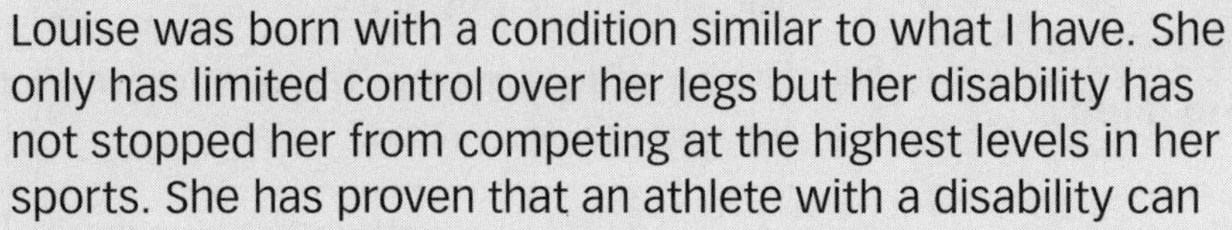

Louise was born with a condition similar to what I have. She only has limited control over her legs but her disability has not stopped her from competing at the highest levels in her sports. She has proven that an athlete with a disability can excel at sport just like an able-bodied athlete. Louise has a great attitude. She has determination and is prepared to work hard. That's why she has been so successful.

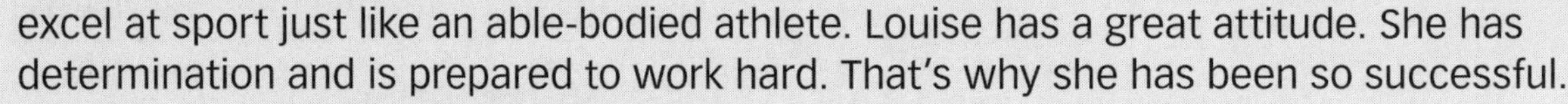

Louise is a role model for all Australians and her great achievements in sport have helped to raise the status of athletes with disabilities.

She tells people that her motto is 'You never know what you can do or achieve until you try.' That's my motto too. By Jonathan

1. Louise Sauvage is the writer's
   - **A** friend.
   - **B** mother.
   - **C** role model.
   - **D** teacher.
2. The writer has a problem with
   - **A** his schoolwork.
   - **B** his legs.
   - **C** playing tennis.
   - **D** his attitude.
3. The photo is of
   - **A** a wheelchair.
   - **B** Lousie Sauvage.
   - **C** Jonathan.
   - **D** the writer's friend.
4. Choose all that apply. Louise Sauvage is
   - **A** an athlete with a disability.
   - **B** Australian.
   - **C** someone the writer knows.
   - **D** a track and field champion.
5. Jonathan is
   - **A** miserable and annoyed.
   - **B** lonely but willing to work hard.
   - **C** positive and happy.
   - **D** hardworking but lacks ambition.
6. How do you think Jonathan's parents would feel if they read his text?
   - **A** worried and sad
   - **B** proud but sad
   - **C** disappointed and annoyed
   - **D** proud and happy

Spelling

Rewrite the misspelt words.

1 Jonathan wants to be a tennis champian.

2 Louise Sauvage is a sucsesfull athlete.

3 Louise is an athlete with a dissabilty.

4 She competes intanationally.

5 Write three words from the word family that includes **competing**.

Vocabulary

Circle the word that has the nearest meaning to the underlined word.

6 Sauvage has proven that an athlete with a disability can excel at sports.
- A tested
- B recognised
- C demonstrated
- D discovered

7 Sauvage has a great attitude.
- A personality
- B decision
- C outlook
- D attempt

8 Add a word from the text to the sentence.
Louise Sauvage is a sporting ______.

9 Write a word from the text to match the meaning.
to manage the use of something

Circle the word on each line that does **not** belong.

10 try surrender endeavour attempt

11 stubbornness weakness determination resolve

Grammar

12 Complete the sentence with a noun group from the text.
Louise Sauvage is ______.

13 Complete the sentence with a saying verb from the text.
She ______ everyone her motto.

14 Complete the sentence with an adverbial phrase.
An athlete ______ can excel at sport.

15 Use a connective from the box to show Jonathan may do one thing or another.

Also	Next	Consequently	Alternatively

Jonathan might become a tennis champion.
______, he might excel in track and field.

Punctuation

16 Circle the sentence that is punctuated correctly.
- A 'That's my motto too' said jonathan.
- B 'That's my motto too,' said Jonathan.
- C 'That's my motto too' said Jonathan.

Rewrite each sentence correctly.

17 louise sauvage is my hero said jonathan

18 theyve got the same motto

Reading and Comprehension

A public service announcement

Name: *Fatima Hassan*

I noticed an advertisement on the television which tried to persuade:

people not to go into floodwater. The ad warned about driving, cycling, playing in floodwater or walking through floodwater. The ad said that floodwater is very powerful even when it doesn't look dangerous. Sometimes drivers think the water looks safe but it can suddenly sweep a car off the road and into a creek or river. The other thing the ad said about floodwater is that it can contain dangerous things like sewage and dead animals, as well as submerged objects.

This ad caught my attention because:

It was scary. I had seen a report on the news where a whole family drowned in their car in floodwater. The driver had attempted to drive across a flooded causeway and the floodwater had swept the car into the river. The family couldn't get out. The reporter announced that it was a tragedy. I thought how scary it would be to be trapped in a car and swept into a river.

The main message of the ad was:

'If it's flooded forget it.'

1 The advertisement attempts to persuade people

- **A** to be careful in floodwater.
- **B** not to go in floodwater.
- **C** not to get drowned in floods.
- **D** that floods are fun.

2 What tragedy had Fatima seen on the news?

- **A** a family driving in floodwater
- **B** a family drowning in floodwater
- **C** a car being swept into a river
- **D** dead animals in floodwater

3 Choose all that apply. How might a submerged object be dangerous?

- **A** It could trap you.
- **B** It could tangle you.
- **C** You don't know it's there.
- **D** You could hit your head on it.

4 Choose all that apply. Dead animals are dangerous in a flood because

- **A** they might knock you over.
- **B** they could bite you.
- **C** they would have germs.
- **D** you might get a fright and drown.

5 Choose all that apply. Do you think the ad was successful?

- **A** No, because Fatima couldn't remember it.
- **B** Yes, because it caught Fatima's attention.
- **C** Yes, because Fatima remembered what the ad was about.
- **D** No, because Fatima didn't care about safety in floodwaters.

6 How can floodwater be dangerous but not look dangerous?

....

....

Spelling

Rewrite the misspelt words.

1 Floodwater is <u>dangerus</u>.

....

2 The ad tried to <u>perswade</u> people.

....

3 The ad <u>cort</u> Fatima's attention.

....

4 There might be <u>submerjed</u> objects.

....

5 Write three words from the word family that includes **water**.

....

....

....

Vocabulary

Circle the word that has the nearest meaning to the underlined word.

6 Floodwater can <u>sweep</u> a car off a road.

A hurry **B** carry
C drive **D** float

7 It's a <u>tragedy</u> when people die unnecessarily.

A problem **B** worry
C concern **D** disaster

8 Add a word from the text to the sentence.

You can't see .... objects.

9 Write a word from the text to match the meaning.

a person who presents news

....

Circle the word on each line that does **not** belong.

10 safe harmless innocent dangerous

11 scary calming frightening terrifying

Grammar

12 Complete the sentence with a noun group from the text.

The family drowned in ....

13 Choose the correct verb to complete the sentence.

Floodwaters (sweep / sweeps) cars off roads.

14 Complete the sentence with an adverbial phrase.

Do not go ....

15 Use a connective from the box to complete the sentence correctly.

also	next	consequently	alternatively

Drive around flooded roads or,

..............................,

stay home.

Punctuation

16 Circle the sentence that is punctuated correctly.

A The police officer said, Don't enter floodwater?

B The police officer said, 'Don't enter floodwater.'

C The police officer said 'Don't enter floodwater.'

Rewrite each sentence correctly.

17 sometimes floodwater doesnt look dangerous

....

....

18 fatimas review was interesting

....

....

Reading and Comprehension

Dancers rule!

The photo is of my sister, Kelsey. She loves dancing and is very talented at it. She has good rhythm and remembers all the steps and moves. She loves dancing to pop songs and sings along as she dances. She knows all the words. She has dance class twice a week.

Mum enrolled Kelsey in dancing classes to help her develop balance and coordination, to get her fitter and healthier and so that she can have fun, make new friends and develop confidence. That last goal has sure worked out the way Mum wanted it to. At the last dance concert, Kelsey had a solo part. She was terrific. Everyone clapped and cheered. Kelsey grinned her head off.

I love to watch Kelsey dance because she enjoys herself so much. The music is good too.

By Justin

Dancers Rule!

Come to our concert
5 pm Wednesday
26 October
Melwood
Community Hall

ALL WELCOME

Please join us in celebrating the wonderful talents of these dancers.
Entry by gold coin donation
Refreshments for sale
Order a program in advance to print at home.

Down Syndrome Association of Melwood

1. What time does the concert start?
   - **A** 26 October
   - **B** 5 pm
   - **C** Wednesday
   - **D** All welcome
2. People clapped and cheered after Kelsey's solo because
   - **A** she grinned her head off.
   - **B** she sang along.
   - **C** she knew all the words to the song.
   - **D** she was terrific.
3. How much does it cost to attend the concert?
   - **A** one dollar
   - **B** at least one dollar
   - **C** more than one dollar
   - **D** 50c
4. Which of Mum's goals has worked out best?
   - **A** to get Kelsey fitter and healthier
   - **B** to help Kelsey's balance and coordination
   - **C** to help Kelsey make new friends
   - **D** to give Kelsey confidence
5. How does Justin feel about his sister's dancing?
   - **A** proud but jealous
   - **B** jealous but loving
   - **C** bored but supportive
   - **D** proud and pleased
6. What does Justin like best about the dancing?
   - **A** the music
   - **B** knowing Kelsey is getting fitter
   - **C** seeing his mum happy
   - **D** watching Kelsey have fun

Spelling

Rewrite the misspelt words.

1 She has good rythm.

2 Dancing helps with coordunation.

3 The dance is on at the communety hall.

4 Dancing helps to develop confudence.

5 Write three words from the word family that includes **celebrating**.

Vocabulary

Circle the word that has the nearest meaning to the underlined word.

6 She is a talented dancer.
   A entertaining   B happy
   C good   D gifted

7 Mum enrolled Kelsey in dance classes.
   A started   B took
   C joined   D enveloped

8 Add a word from the text to the sentence.
   Kelsey can .... on one foot.

9 Write a word from the text to match the meaning.
   to have belief in oneself

Circle the word on each line that does **not** belong.

10 goal aim talent objective

11 solo group solitary single-handed

Grammar

12 Complete the sentence with a noun group from the text.
   Kelsey grinned .... off.

13 Choose the correct verb to complete the sentence.
   Refreshments (are / is) available for purchase.

14 Complete the sentence with an adverbial phrase.
   Mum enrolled Kelsey
   ....

15 Use a connective from the box to complete the sentence correctly.

also	next	consequently	alternatively

Dancing makes you fitter and
....
it's good fun.

Punctuation

16 Circle the sentence that is punctuated correctly.
   A 'Great dancing, Kelsey!' called Justin.
   B 'Great dancing, Kelsey' called justin.
   C 'Great dancing, Kelsey!' called Justin.'

Rewrite each sentences correctly.

17 I love dancing declared kelsey

18 youre a great dancer said mum

Reading and Comprehension

The mysterious machine

Phillip and Noomi had been told to stay out of the garage. Their mum was a scientist. She used to work for the government but she left that job to work at home on what she called 'a personal project'. The children rarely saw her. She'd told their dad she'd had a breakthrough and was really excited about it. The children had stayed away from the garage for months but their curiosity had overtaken their obedience and now here they stood, staring at a strange, whirring machine.

It was similar in shape to a helicopter but it had no blades. It hovered above a spinning base. It had a large front windscreen, two doors and two seats. Inside there was a screen that was flashing a time and a weird date: 18:48 07/10/2089. The machine was attached with wires and cables to a computer on a desk. Computer codes were scrolling on the screen.

'What do you think it is?' asked Phillip.

'Where's Mum?' asked Noomi.

1. Why was the date weird?
   - A It was Noomi's birthday.
   - B It was in the future.
   - C It was not the date of that day.
   - D It wasn't really a date.
2. Choose a description of the machine.
   - A round and whirring
   - B smooth and silent
   - C still and special
   - D solid and bright
3. What was Mum's 'personal project'?
   - A inventing a time machine
   - B inventing a new method of transport
   - C inventing a machine for space travel
   - D inventing a flying saucer
4. Where was Mum?
   - A vanished in space
   - B in the kitchen
   - C back at work
   - D disappeared in time
5. Choose all that apply. Mum is
   - A obsessed with her work.
   - B very smart.
   - C lazy and forgetful.
   - D secretive.
6. What do you think the children will do? Explain.

   ....

   ....

   ....

   ....

Spelling

Rewrite the misspelt words.

1 The machine stood in the garaj.

____

2 Curiosety had overtaken them.

____

3 It had a large front winscreen.

____

4 The mashine had wires attached.

____

5 Write three words from the word family that includes **obedience**.

____

____

____

Vocabulary

Circle the word that has the nearest meaning to the underlined word.

6 The children rarely saw their mother.
- A sometimes
- B frequently
- C often
- D seldom

7 Their curiosity had overtaken them.
- A indifference
- B snooping
- C inquisitiveness
- D meddlesomeness

8 Add a word from the text to the sentence.

The machine ____________ over its base.

9 Write a word from the text to match the meaning.

something odd or unusual

____

Circle the word on each line that does **not** belong.

10 project skill endeavour task

11 indifferent thrilled excited enthusiastic

Grammar

12 Complete the sentence with a noun group from the text.

____________ was a scientist.

13 Choose the correct verb to complete the sentence.

The children (was / were) worried about their mother.

14 Complete the sentence with an adverbial phrase.

It hovered ____________.

15 Use a connective from the box to complete the sentence correctly.

also	next	consequently	alternatively

Mum was a scientist,

____

things in the garage could be dangerous.

Punctuation

16 Circle the sentence that is punctuated correctly.
- A What is it? asked Phillip.
- B 'What is it asked Phillip.'
- C 'What is it?' asked Phillip.

Rewrite each sentence correctly.

17 mum was a scientist and shed had a breakthrough

____

____

____

18 whats happened asked noomi

____

____

____

Book review: *Queenie—One Elephant's Story*

Author: Corinne Fenton Illustrator: Peter Gouldthorpe

This is the true story of an elephant that was born in India in the wild. When she was only little she was captured by hunters and sent by ship to a zoo in Melbourne, Australia. She was named Queenie.

Queenie lived at the zoo for 40 years making crowds of people happy. Zoo visitors loved her. In 1944 she accidentally crushed her keeper so the zoo decided they had to destroy her. Another reason for having Queenie destroyed was that it was during World War II and there were food shortages.

I think this is a sad story. It's not fair that an elephant was stolen from her mother and her herd in the wild to be kept in a zoo for 40 years and then killed. Queenie never got to live the life of a wild elephant or to be with a family. This story tells people how we treated animals in those times.

I recommend this book because it's a true story and it makes people think about captive animals. I think wild animals belong in the wild. By Sigrid

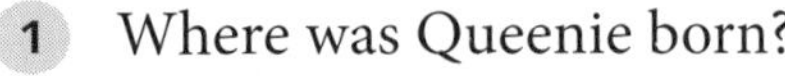

1 Where was Queenie born?
- **A** Melbourne
- **B** Australia
- **C** in a zoo
- **D** India

2 Who captured Queenie?
- **A** a zoo
- **B** hunters
- **C** her keeper
- **D** Melbourne

3 What was Queenie's role at the zoo?
- **A** staff member
- **B** to teach children about elephants
- **C** to entertain
- **D** an exhibit

4 Sigrid thinks the book
- **A** helps people understand what happened to Queenie.
- **B** makes people avoid zoos.
- **C** helps people understand the life of a zoo animal.
- **D** makes people love elephants.

5 Does Sigrid believe that destroying Queenie was the right thing to do?
- **A** Yes. There was no food for her.
- **B** Yes. She might have crushed someone else.
- **C** No. It wasn't fair.
- **D** No. Sigrid would have taken her home.

6 Australian law now states that animals can no longer be taken from the wild for zoos. What do you think about that?

....

....

....

Spelling

Rewrite the misspelt words.

1 Queenie was an elefant.

2 Queenie was capchured in India.

3 I reckammend this book.

4 The keeper was aksadently crushed.

5 Write three words from the word family that includes **destroy**.

Vocabulary

Circle the word that has the nearest meaning to the underlined word.

6 Queenie was destroyed.

A dead B captured
C loved D killed

7 There was a shortage of food.

A abundance B deficiency
C excess D over-supply

8 Add a word from the text to the sentence.

The ______ is Peter Gouldthorpe.

9 Write a word from the text to match the meaning.

large gatherings of people

Circle the word on each line that does **not** belong.

10 cage enclosure wild tank

11 stolen taken thieved returned

Grammar

12 Complete the sentence with a noun group from the text.

Queenie never got to live with ______.

13 Choose the correct verb to complete the sentence.

The herd of elephants (live / lives) in India.

14 Complete the sentence with an adverbial phrase.

Queenie was stolen ______.

15 Add the correct pronoun to complete the sentence.

also	next	consequently	alternatively

Queenie crushed her keeper. For doing this ______ was killed.

Punctuation

16 Circle the sentence that is punctuated correctly.

A The Author is Corinne Fenton.
B The author is Corinne Fenton.
C The Author is Corinne Fenton

17 Rewrite each sentence correctly.

queenie lived in a zoo in Melbourne

18 think about captive animals said sigrid

Reading and Comprehension

Write a common noun from the box in each space.

herds	zoos	medals	hunters	coordination
athlete	balance	animals	Australia	wild

1 Louise Sauvage is an ____________ who has won ____________ competing for ____________.

2 Elephants live in ____________ in the ____________. In the past, Australian ____________ bought ____________ that had been captured by ____________ in the wild.

3 Dancing is good for ____________ and ____________.

Write a word from the box in each space.

disabilities	animals	energetic	juices	swiftly
submerged	foods	machine	dangerous	flooded

4 Floodwater is ____________. Floodwater can move ____________. Floodwater can hide ____________ objects such as dead ____________. The message is 'If it's ____________ forget it.'

5 The cafe serves healthy ____________ and beverages such as vegetable ____________ to keep you feeling ____________.

6 A rehabilitation pool is used by people with ____________.

7 A time ____________ would be an amazing invention.

Spelling

The spelling mistakes in these sentences have been circled. Write the correct spelling on the lines.

8 The children (arived) at school. ____________

9 The little pool is (suitible) for toddlers. ____________

10 The cafe sells (vegtable) juice. ____________

11 Advertisements try to (perswade) people. ____________

12 The concert is in the (communety) hall. ____________

13 Dance is a (celabration). ____________

14 Our bikes are in the (garaije) with the car. ____________

15 A computer is a useful (mashine). ____________

Vocabulary

16 Circle the correct word in the brackets.
The dog peered (threw / through) the fence.

17 Circle the word that means the opposite of **goal**.
aim result objective

Grammar

18 Add a noun to the sentence.
Louise Sauvage is an Australian ____________________.

19 Add an adverbial to the sentence.
Some athletes ____________________ for their country.

20 Add an adverbial phrase to tell **where**.
Swimming training takes place ____________________.

21 Add a pronoun to the sentence.
The children looked everywhere but ____________________ could not find their mother.

22 Add a connective to the sentence.
Jonathan might do swimming ____________________ he could take up dancing.

Punctuation

Rewrite each sentence correctly.

23 great dancing keith called nicole

____

____

24 whats happened to mum asked noomi

____

____

25 thats a great story said darcey

____

____

NAPLAN-STYLE

4

READING TEST

Reading

We've been robbed!

Scarlet and Isaac meandered home from school. They turned onto their own road and immediately noticed a police car parked in Isaac's driveway.

They looked at each other, Scarlet seeing the worry in Isaac's eyes. Then they took off.

The children burst through the front door to find Isaac's home in a huge mess. It had been trashed. All the family's things had been tossed off shelves, out of drawers and onto the floor.

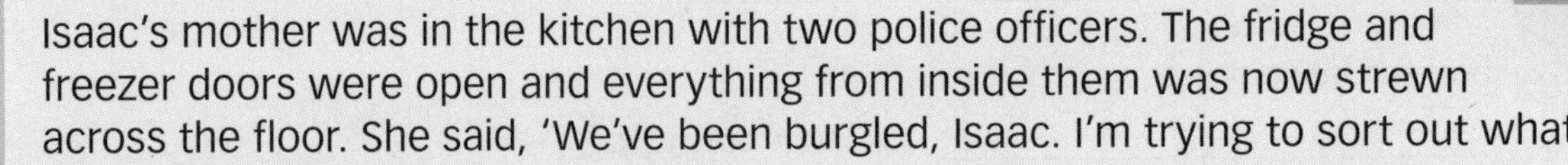

Isaac's mother was in the kitchen with two police officers. The fridge and freezer doors were open and everything from inside them was now strewn across the floor. She said, 'We've been burgled, Isaac. I'm trying to sort out what's been taken. Go and look in your room and tell me if anything is missing.'

Rushing to his room, Isaac went straight to his wardrobe to check his new soccer ball. Yes. It was still there. He sighed with relief as he looked at Scarlet. He hated the thought of a robber stealing his new soccer ball.

His drawers had been upended onto the floor but he didn't have any money in them or anything else valuable. Then he noticed his undies scattered across the floor. He felt his face flush red.

1 Where had Scarlet and Isaac been?
- A at the park
- B at home
- C at school
- D in Isaac's driveway

2 Where was the police car?
- A on the road
- B in the driveway
- C on the footpath
- D at the police station

3 When he saw the police car, Isaac would have been most worried about
- A a fire.
- B a robbery.
- C his mother.
- D his soccer ball.

4 What might robbers have hoped to find in Isaac's drawers?
- A clothes
- B schoolwork
- C money
- D food

5 What relationship do Scarlet and Isaac have?
- A brother and sister
- B friends
- C cousins
- D mother and son

6 Why was food tipped onto the floor?
- A The burglar was looking for hidden valuables.
- B The burglar was hungry.
- C The burglar stole good food.
- D The burglar wanted to make a mess.

7 Why did Isaac's face flush red?
- A He was annoyed about the burglary.
- B He was pleased his soccer ball was safe.
- C He was angry that his room was a mess.
- D He was embarrassed in front of Scarlet.

NAPLAN-STYLE 4 CONVENTIONS OF LANGUAGE TEST

Spelling

The spelling mistakes in these sentences have been underlined. Write the correct spelling on the lines.

1 The children birst through the front door. ______________________

2 The socca ball was safe. ______________________

3 His undies were scatterd across the floor. ______________________

4 The burglar wanted valubles. ______________________

Vocabulary

5 Which word means **to be robbed**?

A burgled B stolen C robber D thief

6 Which word does **not** belong?

A meandered B raced C strolled D dawdled

7 Which word does **not** belong?

A burglar B robber C police D criminal

Grammar

8 Which adjective describes Isaac's home?

A tidy B busy C crowded D messy

9 Which words complete the sentence?

A police car ______________________ by the children.

A did notice B was noticed C were noticing D noticed

10 Which adverb completes the sentence to tell **how**?

Isaac raced home ______________________.

A urgent B slowly C urgently D quicker

Punctuation

11 Which sentence is punctuated correctly?

A What's missing? asked Mum

B 'Look in your room, said Mum'

C 'Why is there such a mess?' asked Isaac.

D What's going on? Asked Mum.

12 Which sentence is punctuated correctly?

A 'What a mess!' Said Isaac.

B 'What a mess!' said Scarlet.

C 'I am so upset said Mum.'

D 'Well' find the thief.'

Reprinted 2019, 2020, 2021, 2022

Updated in 2024 for the NSW Curriculum and Australian Curriculum Version 9.0 changes

ISBN 978 1 74125 612 3

Pascal Press
PO Box 250
Glebe NSW 2037
(02) 9198 1748
www.pascalpress.com.au

Publisher: Vivienne Joannou
Project editors: Rosemary Peers and Mark Dixon
Edited by Rosemary Peers and Mark Dixon
Answers checked by Glenda Walsh
Cover and page design by Kim Webber
Typeset by Julianne Billington (lj Design) and Leanne Richters (Grizzly Graphics)
Printed by Vivar Printing/Green Giant Press